W9-DDU-114

Canadian Concepts 6

Lynda Berish
Sandra Thibaudeau

Prentice Hall Canada Inc., Scarborough, Ontario

Canadian Cataloguing in Publication Data

Berish, Lynda, 1952–
Canadian concepts 6

ISBN 0-13-184904-2

1. English language – Textbooks for second language learners.* 2. English language – Grammar.
3. English language – Problems, exercises, etc.
I. Thibaudeau, Sandra, 1943– . II. Title.

PE1128.B47 1993   428.2`4   C93-094285-X

Prentice-Hall, Inc., Englewood Cliffs, New Jersey
Prentice-Hall International, Inc., London
Prentice-Hall of Australia, Pty., Ltd., Sydney
Prentice-Hall of India Pvt., Ltd., New Delhi
Prentice-Hall of Japan, Inc., Tokyo
Prentice-Hall of Southeast Asia (Pte.) Ltd., Singapore
Editora Prentice-Hall do Brasil Ltda., Rio de Janeiro
Prentice-Hall Hispanoamericana, S.A., Mexico

ISBN 0-13-184904-2

Acquisitions editor: Joe March
Coordinating editor: Karen Sacks
Production editor: Elynor Kagan
Production coordinator: Anita Boyle
Design and layout: Joseph Chin
Illustrations: Paul McCusker
Audio cassettes: Morris Apelbaum,
              Silent Sound Studio, Montreal
Cover design: Aurora Di Ciaula
Cover illustration: June Bradford

 2 3 4 5   97 96 95 94

Printed and bound in Canada

The authors would like to acknowledge, with thanks, the organizations, publications and individuals who gave permission to reprint information they have published.

"They're Not Tremblays and They're Not Smiths" by Debbie Parkes reprinted by permission of *The Gazette,* Montreal.

"Peanut Butter at 100 Still Loves Jelly" by Dena Kleiman, April 14, 1990. Copyright © 1990 by The New York Times Company. Reprinted by permission.

"Will China Embrace the Fortune Cookie?" by Sheryl WuDunn, April 5, 1989. Copyright © 1989 by The New York Times Company. Reprinted by permission.

"Fire Safety" by C.D. Clark reprinted by permission of Price Club.

Information from the *Canadian Red Cross Passport to Safety* reprinted with permission of the Canadian Red Cross Society, Quebec Division.

"In Times Gone By" reprinted by permission of Joanne Mills.

"From tubas to peg legs: air travellers have lost it all" by David Gersovitz reprinted by permission of The Canadian Press.

"Travelling Light" by Kathleen Doheny reprinted by permission of the *Los Angeles Times.*

"Night Work" by Sandy Bauers reprinted by permission of the Knight-Ridder/Tribune News Service.

"Family Lies" by Marsha Skuce reprinted by permission of the *Ottawa Citizen.*

"Money Makes the World Go Around" reprinted by permission of the *Royal Bank Reporter.*

Contents

To the Teacher

The *Canadian Concepts* Series

The *Canadian Concepts* Series is a six-book series designed for students learning English in Canada. Survival topics and cultural information based on Canadian themes help students integrate into the community. The themes are recycled with increasing complexity throughout the series. Practical topics in the lower levels progress to topics of interest and concern to more advanced students.

The *Canadian Concepts* Series is communicative in approach. The method offers productive strategies for language learning based on student-centred interaction. The pedagogical model presents students with challenging input, and provides activities that involve the students in information exchange. Students are often asked to work in pairs or groups to extend their understanding through interaction. Fluency activities are supported with spelling, dictation, pronunciation and writing tasks that focus on accuracy.

Canadian Concepts 6

Students using *Canadian Concepts 6* are challenged by exposure to information-rich language. Authentic materials are included in the reading, listening and video activities. Students are asked to perform a variety of tasks designed to improve their skills and language knowledge. Cultural information encourages students to feel at ease while integrating into the community. Students are motivated to interact outside the classroom through Community Contact Tasks.

Teachers and students will appreciate the simplicity of the materials. The clear and attractive layout and illustrations make texts inviting and lend support to the tasks and activities students are asked to perform.

The Units

Canadian Concepts 6 is divided into 12 self-contained units. The units focus on both Canadian and international themes on a variety of current topics, and all include authentic listening and/or reading material.

Each unit offers a wide range of activities which include two or three core activities. These core activities are developed on a model of pre-activity, main task and follow-up activity. Attention is paid to developing productive strategies and to recycling information through different stages.

The Activities

The Teacher's Manual provides suggestions for warm-up activities to use before the students open their books. In the text, the "Get Ready" sections provide reading, listening or video preparation. These pre-activities introduce the topic and generate interest in a variety of ways: through prediction exercises, quizzes, discussion questions, dictation or interaction based on illustrations.

Core activities focus on taped passages, authentic interviews, video presentations, and reading passages that include authentic brochures and newspaper articles. The tasks promote strategies of guessing from context, trying out possible answers and revising understanding through successive steps. Core activities consist of a variety of tasks: reading, listening or viewing for general information; reading, listening or viewing for detailed information; and using the information for speaking, writing or information-transfer tasks.

Follow-up activities recycle language in the unit, providing opportunities for students to express themselves orally, review vocabulary, practise grammar and write.

Pre-Activities	Core Activities	Review and Recycle	Real-Life Application
Get Ready to Read	Read for General Ideas	Review Vocabulary	Exchange Information
Get Ready to Listen	Read for Details	Review Expressions	Discuss
Get Ready to Discuss	Read for Information	Dictation	Give a Report
Get Ready to Watch the Video	Read Quickly to Check Predictions	Tell the Story	Write
Discuss	Read to Increase Speed	Write the Story	Role Play
	Listen for Meaning	Practise Numbers	Community Contact Tasks
	Listen for Details	Transfer Information	
	Watch the Video for General Ideas		
	Watch the Video for Details		

Key to Symbols

[○ ○]	Listening Activity	□ □	Work with a Partner
📖	Reading Activity	⊞	Work in a Group
✏	Writing Activity	😊😢	Role Play
📺	Video Activity		

Listening Programme

The listening programme in *Canadian Concepts 6* consists of a variety of recorded passages. There are scripted listening passages on diverse topics, and authentic interviews on a variety of subjects. Students listen to each passage several times in order to move through different stages of comprehension. Complete listening scripts are provided in the Teacher's Manual.

Video Programme

The video programme consists of three videos, each of which is about 20 minutes long. The activities in units that have this component are built around the content of the videos, so that students are prepared to benefit fully from the video when they view it. Video activities appear at the end of units, and may be omitted without disrupting the continuity of the material if video facilities are not available.

The videos have been selected from the *National Geographic Educational Series*. If they are not available in the library of your institution, the videos can be purchased directly from the National Geographic Society, Educational Services, 211 Watline Avenue, Mississauga, Ontario L4Z 1P3 (Telephone 416-890 1111).

The videos used in *Canadian Concepts 6* are:

The Kingdom of Plants: How Plants Are Used (Video Activity 1, Unit 2)

Dolphins (Video Activity 2, Unit 6)

The Robotics Revolution (Video Activity 3, Unit 10)

Supplementary Grammar

Suggestions for introducing grammar points are given in the Teacher's Manual. Practice exercises and answer keys are also included in the manual. The exercises in the Supplementary Grammar section recycle and reinforce vocabulary from units of the book.

Community Contact Tasks

The Community Contact Tasks are designed to complement activities done in class. Each task is linked to a specific unit in the book. Students are encouraged to practise their English in real-life situations outside the classroom. A variety of tasks has been provided so that a selection can be made according to the needs and interests of the students in a particular class. Worksheets are provided in the Teacher's Manual.

Teacher's Manual

Each book in the series has its own Teacher's Manual that includes:

- step-by-step instructions keyed to the student's book;

- suggestions for classroom interaction;

- answers for exercises;

- tape scripts for listening activities;

- teacher's scripts for dictations and pronunciation exercises;

- photocopying masters of student worksheets for listening activities, video activities, information exchange and Community Contact Tasks.

Detailed teacher's notes are included to make the intention of activities clear and to guide new teachers. Experienced teachers will find that the material is flexible and accommodates individual teaching styles. Teachers can easily supplement thematic units with current authentic material they find appropriate.

The authors wish success to their colleagues and the students who use these Canadian materials.

Lynda Berish
Sandra Thibaudeau

Acknowledgements

We are grateful for the support of a number of people in the classroom testing of the materials in this book. We would like to thank colleagues and students at the Centre for Continuing Education at Concordia University: Della Yaxley, Nicole Lachance, Claude Lefrançois, Caroline Guibbert, Chantal Razafindrabe, Alam Ashraful, Hida Hisaki, François Meunier, Thillayampalam Thavaputhiran, Victor Singh, Ping He, Monica Zapata, Joan Subirachs-Roig, Ahmad A.N. Magdoub, Edward Szczepara, and Salemi Sangali.

We thank many colleagues in the field for their continued support as well, particularly Geoff Blake of Columbia College, Edna Downey of CEGEP St. Jerome, Maria De Rosa Wilson of Language Studies Canada, and Lawrence Keenan of CSLI. We would also like to thank Pie-Yuan Han for his support.

Very special thanks go to Nina Peritz for contributing her time and her excellent interviewing skills. Her expertise helped make the interviews lively and informative. We offer special thanks also to the following people for lending their time and expertise for the interviews: Richard Goldman, Debra Finestone M.D., Lynn Johnston, and Joanne Mills. Their knowledge and experience provided us with valuable information and stimulating ideas.

We would like to express appreciation to several people who have offered particular encouragement in the *Canadian Concepts* project: Jerry Smith, Yolanda de Rooy, Joe March, Kedre Murray, Marjorie Walker, Linda Gorman, and Karen Sacks. We would also like to express thanks for the technical expertise provided by Morris Apelbaum and Joe Chin, and for the invaluable editorial assistance of Elynor Kagan.

Our thanks go also to our families for the patience and help they have extended: to our husbands, John Berish and Charles Gruss, and to our children, Tara and Andrea Berish and Jean-Baptiste, Gabrielle and Annabel Thibaudeau. Thanks also to Howard Berish for his advice and assistance, and to Max and Millicent Goldman who, over many years and in many ways, have offered the kind of encouragement writers need to keep going.

The World

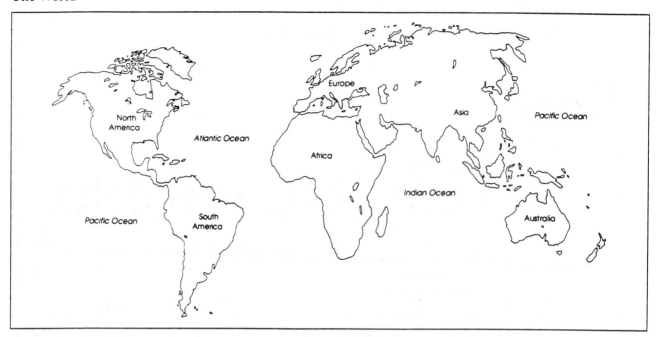

Canada

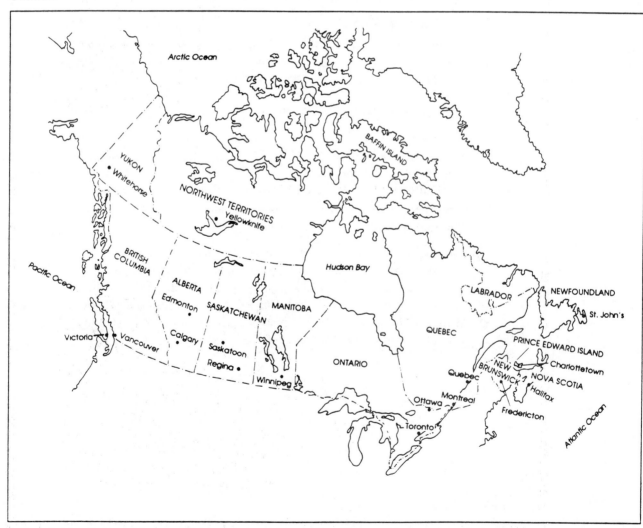

Meeting People

Customs Quiz
Interaction
Cultural Information

Coffee and Doughnuts
Listening Activity 1

Can You Remember?
Spelling

What Do You Say?
Discussion
Cultural Information

The Process of Elimination
Interaction

They're Not Tremblays and They're Not Smiths
Reading
Cultural Information

About You
Writing

Customs Quiz

What do you know about customs in different countries? Discuss these questions in a group.
Choose the best answers.

1. In which country is punctuality very important?
   a) Brazil
   b) Sweden
   c) the Philippines

2. When someone says "Thank you," the appropriate answer is:
   a) "You're welcome."
   b) "Huh?"
   c) "Come again?"

3. When you call your friend, you hear a message from a telephone answering machine. It is appropriate to:
   a) bang down the receiver
   b) leave your name and number
   c) tell a joke

4. In China, which of these is not a good gift?
   a) shoes
   b) a clock
   c) flowers

5. If someone asks you "What's up?", they want to know:
   a) about your plans
   b) about the weather
   c) about your hair

6. If someone asks you "What do you say to a cup of coffee?", the answers could be:
   a) "Hi coffee!"
   b) "No thanks."
   c) "Sure."

7. In which language is "Salud" a toast?
   a) German
   b) Russian
   c) Spanish

8. Which colour is never worn at Japanese weddings?
   a) red
   b) purple
   c) white

9. When someone from Indonesia asks you "Where are you going?", the appropriate response is:
   a) "It's none of your business."
   b) "Where are you going?"
   c) "Just for a walk."

10. In which country is an orchid most appreciated as a gift?
    a) Venezuela
    b) Canada
    c) India

11. Where do people eat with the fork in the left hand and the knife in the right hand?

    a) North America

    b) Europe

    c) Asia

12. In which country is belching after a meal considered a compliment to the cook?

    a) Taiwan

    b) Turkey

    c) Mexico

13. In which country do children celebrate their name days (saint's feast days) rather than their birthdays?

    a) France

    b) Paraguay

    c) Britain

14. Who would be addressed as "Your Royal Highness"?

    a) a king

    b) a queen

    c) a judge

15. In Canada, most people address each other by:

    a) first names

    b) last names

    c) first and last names

16. In which of these countries would you be most likely to get a hug as a greeting?

    a) Britain

    b) Japan

    c) Mexico

17. If you want a server's attention in a restaurant in Canada, you should:

    a) try to catch his or her eye

    b) snap your fingers

    c) yell "Waiter!"

18. In which country should you take off your shoes before entering a house?

    a) Japan

    b) Canada

    c) England

19. When a European asks "How are you?", the appropriate response is:

    a) "Fine."

    b) "I have a cold."

    c) "Not so good. You see..."

20. In Australia, your "mate" is your:

    a) husband or wife

    b) sister or brother

    c) friend

21. If someone asks you "How's it going?", an appropriate response would be:

    a) "To the library."

    b) "OK"

    c) "How are you?"

22. In Canada, when you finish eating a chocolate bar, you should:

    a) put the wrapper in your pocket

    b) put the wrapper in the garbage

    c) throw the wrapper on the ground

23. Which of these is considered bad luck as a gift in many European countries?

    a) an even number of flowers

    b) an unwrapped bouquet

    c) an uneven number of flowers

24. If you visit someone's house in Canada, you should:

    a) leave right after the meal

    b) stay for a while

    c) ask if you can stay overnight

Coffee and Doughnuts

Listening Activity 1

Exercise 1: Get Ready to Listen

Discuss these questions in a group.

1. Do you drink coffee? How do you take it?
2. Name some types of coffee.
3. What are some of the things people take in their coffee?
4. What are some of the times when people traditionally drink coffee?
5. Name some foods people like to eat when they drink coffee.

Exercise 2: Listen for Meaning

Listen to the information. What is the main idea of this passage?

a) different kinds of coffee

b) the popularity of coffee

c) where people drink coffee

Exercise 3: Listen for Details

Listen to the information. While you listen, answer the questions.

1. Who drinks 3.75 cups of coffee a day?

2. How many cups of coffee are drunk in Canada annually?

3. When do some people not like to drink coffee?

4. Who are the biggest consumers of coffee?

5. What do people eat with coffee in the morning? After dinner?

6. Name some ways to prepare coffee.

7. Where do people go to drink coffee outside their homes?

8. What is part of the business of a coffee shop?

9. What is a "regular"?

10. Name some of the types of people you can meet in a coffee shop.

11. Who takes coffee breaks in the office?

12. What is a coffee pool?

13. What is replacing the term "coffee break" in some places?

14. Compare the number of doughnut shops in Canada with the number in the rest of the world.

15. Support the statement, "Coffee is a very big industry."

Exercise 4: Tell the Story

Explain the information to a partner. Use your own words.

Can You Remember?

One way to remember facts, rules or ideas is by rhyming. Read this rhyme and then apply the spelling rule to the list of words your teacher reads you.

I before E

Except after C

Or when sounded like A

As in "neighbour" and "weigh"

What Do You Say?

What do you say in each of these circumstances? Work in a group to discuss what you can say when:

1. you don't understand what someone is saying
2. you want to invite someone to sit down with you
3. you want to pass someone in a narrow space
4. you are with a group of people and you want to smoke
5. you want someone to go through a doorway before you
6. someone near you sneezes
7. you hand a paper to someone
8. someone mentions that it is her birthday
9. someone is about to walk into something
10. you learn that a friend's father has died
11. you want to offer someone a seat on a bus
12. someone is wanted on the phone
13. you want to know the time and don't have a watch
14. you don't agree with what someone is saying
15. you need to borrow someone's umbrella to go out for a minute
16. you want to signal a server in a restaurant
17. someone pushes into line in front of you
18. you get a wrong number on the telephone

Do You Know Jane and John Doe?

This couple has been around since the 1300s and is still going strong. The names "Jane" and "John" were chosen as the most common first names of those early times. The names are still used today by people who wish to remain anonymous, or to refer to someone whose identity is unknown.

The Process of Elimination

□ □ Work with a partner. Use this information to find the profession of each woman.

Three young women, Michiko, Maria and Gaby, live next door to each other in an apartment building. Maria lives between her two friends. One woman works as a model, one as a decorator and one as a journalist. The decorator walks Gaby's dog when she goes on holiday. The journalist taps on Michiko's wall when her TV is too loud.

They're Not Tremblays and They're Not Smiths

Exercise 1: Get Ready to Read

□ □ Read the title above. It matches the title of the newspaper article on page 8. Read the paragraph below. Then tell your partner what you think the article will be about.

Until recent times, many of the people living in Canada were descendants of the early French or British settlers. The most common name in French Canada was Tremblay. The most common name among English Canadians was Smith. Of course, there were many Native Canadians and immigrants from other countries who had their own names that were nothing like Smith or Tremblay. Today, Canada's population is increasingly diverse, and knowing your neighbours' names is getting trickier.

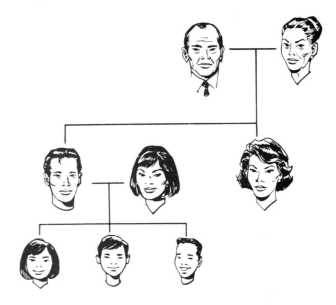

They're not Tremblays and They're not Smiths

Debbie Parkes

The Gazette, Montreal

Meet Michael Baffoe, the son of Kwaku Esson and Ama Baduaa. Baffoe has brothers and sisters but they don't share his second name. And neither do his parents. "We do not carry a name through the family," says Baffoe, a member of the Akan tribe of Ghana. He gets a kick out of the confusion this causes to most Canadians. How do you know who is related to whom? "You have to ask," Baffoe says.

Here's something else to mull over the next time you pour yourself a coffee: Many Akans carry a name that indicates the day of the week they were born—and/or their position in the family. Take Baffoe's father's name, Kwaku Esson. Kwaku tells you he was born on a Wednesday. Esson tells you he was the seventh born.

There's a whole set of names based on the days of the week—one for males, the other for females. Spellings vary somewhat according to the spoken dialect. More and more, says Baffoe, Ghanaians are adopting western names—wherefore Michael. But at home, he says, he is called by his Akan name, Kofi. And if you're up on your Akan, you know right away that Baffoe was born on a Friday.

Can keep names

People born in Canada must be registered with at least one given name and a family name—the latter either that of the mother or the father, or a combination of the two. But immigrants are allowed to keep the names they had when coming here.

Baffoe isn't alone among Canadians with unconventional names—at least unconventional to Canadians who have been here longer. Take Muhammad Hedayetullah, a native of Bangladesh. When he first landed in Montreal 25 years ago, the Muhammad wasn't part of his name. That changed the day he registered at McGill University.

The lady at the counter asked his name. "Hedayetullah," he replied quite correctly, that being the only one he had. But she wanted a "Christian" name. A friend in line tactfully told the woman: "He's Muslim." So after a brief argument, he gave her "Muhammad" and he's stuck with that ever since.

But Hedayetullah is not the name you will hear him referred to among family members in Bangladesh. "Almost everyone has a call name in our country," say Hedayetullah. "That call name is never used outside family and close friends." But he won't reveal what his is. To do so is taboo.

"Royal origin"

Nam Nguyen of Vietnam has altered his name for usage among non-Vietnamese Canadians. In its original form, it's Nguyen Van Hoang Nam. As with Chinese and Hungarian names, the family name goes first.

He warns against referring to Vietnamese by their last name only. The vast majority of Vietnamese have one of about seven last names, so any last name is bound to be shared by tens of thousands of individuals.

Hoang Nam, his given name, means "boy of royal origin." In Canada, he drops all mention of royalty, but keeps Nam. He's also dropped the Van. Van is an optional addition to a name that tells you the person is male.

For females, the descriptive name to add, if one wants, is Thi. One can always tell from a Vietnamese given name whether a person is male or female, Nam explains.

Hyphen optional

In China, given names often have two parts, or syllables, with one of them common to family members of the same generation. Often the male head of a family will choose a name to be used with his son's children, says K.C. Woo of the Chinese Community United Centre. Many families have an ancestors' book which lists names for each generation. Sometimes the custom

is carried out for both sexes. Other times it's used only for the males.

Woo puts her husband's family name last to conform to Canadian practice and goes by the name K.C. But her Chinese name is Woo Tse Kam Chu. Tse is her maiden name. Her sister also has Kam in her given name, Kam-Chung. It's up to the individual whether to hyphenate the two syllables and whether to capitalize the second one, says Woo....

Check almanac

Traditionally, Hindu Tamil males have only one name, but in writing, it's preceded by the father's initial. In Canada, so many of the people K. Kasivisvanathan meets expect him to have both first and family names that he gives his father's name, Kathigasoo, as his given name. He uses his own name as a surname.

Tamil girls and women use their own initial before their father's name if they are single, or before that of their husband if they are married. Kasi's wife, Kumarachelvy, signs her name K. Kasivisvanathan.

Another tradition is to check a Tamil almanac and astrological calendar before choosing a name for a newborn child. Most often, says Kasi, parents name a child after a Hindu god or goddess, a custom believed to provide the child extra protection. Explains Kasi: A deity will be summoned each time the child's name is mentioned.

Do You Know Joe?	"Joe" is one of the nicknames used when one man greets another. "Mac," "Jack" and "Bud" are also used, but "Joe" is the most popular. The expression "an average Joe" is sometimes used to represent the everyday man-in-the-street.

Exercise 3: Read Carefully for Details

Work with a partner. Look in the text for the answers.

1. What is confusing to most Canadians about Akan names?
2. What can you tell from an Akan name?
3. Name two things the name Kwaku Esson tells about the person.
4. When was Kofi Baffoe born?
5. How did Hedayetullah get the name Muhammad?
6. Why won't Hedayetullah tell the writer his call name?
7. Why is it hard to know who a Vietnamese is by the family name?
8. Which parts of his name does Nguyen Van Hoang Nam not use in Canada?
9. Which Vietnamese names indicate whether a person is male or female?
10. How many syllables do Chinese given names have?
11. What is an ancestor book?
12. Who decides whether a person should write his or her name with a hyphen?
13. How do Hindu Tamil males traditionally write their names?
14. Explain the naming custom for Tamil girls and women.
15. Name two ways Tamils choose names for a child.
16. According to Tamil tradition, what will happen each time a child's name is called?

Exercise 4: Review Vocabulary

Find words or expressions in the text that mean the same as those below.

1. to be amused by
2. to think about
3. the last thing mentioned
4. arrived
5. has kept
6. forbidden
7. is certain to be
8. to be the same as
9. unmarried
10. be called

Exercise 5: Use the Information

Work in pairs. Choose three of the naming customs discussed in the article and write what your name would be in that culture. Then, exchange lists with your partner and check to see whether you have applied the rules correctly.

About You

Write about yourself. Choose information you would like to share with other people you have just met.

Unit 2

Foods from Far and Near

Peanut Butter: It Won't Grow Up

Exercise 1: Get Ready to Read

Discuss these questions in a group.

1. What are some common foods that people bring to school or work for lunch?

2. What are some foods people take on a picnic or when they are camping out?

3. What kind of sandwiches do you think are the most popular in North America?

4. Do you ever eat peanut butter? How?

Exercise 2: Read Quickly for General Ideas

Read the text quickly. Which of these is the main idea?

a) where peanuts come from originally

b) different ways in which peanut butter can be used

c) cooking traditions around the world

Did You Know?   The fastest way to lose your appetite is to have a good meal!

Peanut Butter: It Won't Grow Up

Dena Kleiman
New York Times

Enough of this kid stuff. Now that peanut butter is 100 years old, let's face facts and stop beating around the bush. Isn't it time for peanut butter to grow up?

It is almost embarrassing to admit. But we North Americans are still serving most of our peanut butter with jelly when so many other parts of the world are using it subtly to enhance stews, thicken soups, or top grilled fish. Isn't it time to start thinking of peanut butter in terms of finesse and fine crystal?

"Beyond the cookie," commanded Ellen Brown, a food consultant, who, as part of peanut butter's 100th anniversary celebration, timistically unveiled 30 new recipes recently at the International Association of Culinary Professionals in Atlanta in the hopes that a more sophisticated image will emerge.

Her creations include recipes for peanut-butter salad dressing, sauces, stews and soups.

There is disagreement about the origin of peanut butter. Some attribute its creation to a St. Louis physician whose identity is not known: others to a man named Joseph Lambert, who ran a nut business out of Battle Creek, Mich. But both are said to have emerged with their creations in the year 1890 and the process was patented seven years later. It became commercially available around the turn of the century.

George Washington Carver, who in 1925 published a paper at Tuskeegee Institute titled "Bulletin No. 31, How to Grow the Peanut and 105 Ways of Preparing It for Human Consumption" is credited with being among the first to concoct the peanut-butter sandwich.

Now peanut butter is among North America's most popular foods, with annual sales of an estimated 800 million pounds a year, said Mitch Head, a spokesman for the Peanut Advisory Commission, a trade association based in Atlanta. An estimated 85 per cent of households have a jar stashed away in a cupboard, he said.

But to keep this in perspective, the peanut is believed to have been first cultivated 1,000 years ago in South America. It was eventually taken to Africa and Asia in the 16th century by explorers from Europe.

Today the peanut and peanut butter are prominently featured in many cuisines. In Thailand, for example, they are used in the preparation of sauces and noodle dishes. In Indonesia, they are the base for a dipping sauce served with chicken and pork dishes.

The peanut is served in soups and stews in African countries like Ghana—where it is combined with tomatoes, onions, eggplant and okra in a stew-like chicken preparation—and in Senegal, where it is combined with sweet potatoes and cabbage. In the Szechuan province of China, it is commonly served in sauces that top noodles and cold chicken.

It is not that these more sophisticated uses of the peanut, which has long been appreciated as an inexpensive source of protein, never occurred to a North American. Indeed Evan Jones, the food historian and author of *American Food: The*

Gastronomic Story (Vintage Books, 1981), said George Washington Carver tried valiantly to show North Americans the many subtle joys of the peanut.

But today the majority of us—58 per cent—continue to prefer our peanut butter on bread, according to research done by CPC International, which manufactures Skippy brand peanut butter. Some 14 per cent prefer it on crackers, while another 10 per cent eat it out of the jar. It is not surprising then to discover that Dr. Peter McCann, a 37-year-old Manhattan surgeon, an otherwise sophisticated diner and exacting food aficionado, prefers his peanut butter on white bread with jelly so thick it leaks through the other side.

Interviews with peanut-butter lovers revealed that, like McCann, many share rather uninhibited childlike delight in the spread. Larry Zisman, for example, who is co-author with his wife, Honey, of the *The Great American Peanut Butter Book* (St. Martin's Press, 1985), said he, too, often eats his peanut butter on bread. His favorite combination, he said, is "putting some peanut butter in your mouth, adding chocolate chips and chewing them together." Frank Treadway, 61, of Fort Meyers, Fla., prefers it "with meat loaf, bacon, cheese and cold baked beans." Norma Carpenter, a 45-year-old Idaho homemaker, routinely eats peanut butter mixed with margarine on popcorn.

Other common ways of eating peanut butter are with apples, celery sticks and bacon, and combined with mayonnaise, pickles, pretzels, corn chips, chocolate pudding, grilled cheese, graham crackers, saltines and whole-wheat toast.

All this may simply mean that peanut butter has just not been around long enough. Maturity, after all, has as much to do with experience as age; not to mention the desire to grow up. Perhaps it should come as no surprise that one of North America's leading brands of peanut butter is called Peter Pan.

Exercise 3: Read Carefully for Details

Work with a partner. Look in the text for the answers.

1. How is peanut butter most often used in North America?
2. What are some ways peanut butter is used in other parts of the world?
3. Why did Ellen Brown unveil 30 new peanut-butter recipes?
4. When was peanut butter patented?
5. How much peanut butter is sold in North America every year?
6. Where was the peanut first grown?
7. How is peanut butter used in Thailand?
8. Where is the peanut used with sweet potatoes and cabbage?
9. What did George Washington Carver try to show North Americans?
10. Name three ways North Americans prefer to eat peanut butter.
11. How does Dr. Peter McCann like to eat peanut butter?
12. How does Larry Zisman prefer to eat peanut butter?
13. Name some other ways peanut butter is eaten in North America.

From Pasta to Pineapples

Listening Activity 2

Exercise 1: Get Ready to Listen

Match the foods on the list with the clues below. Use each food only once.

**chocolate   watermelon   pineapple   spaghetti
milk   olive   banana   ice cream**

1. a white beverage
2. a sweet treat, often made with milk
3. a large fruit, red inside, with many seeds
4. a sweet fruit that is prickly on the outside
5. a food you eat with tomato or meat sauce
6. a small green or black food, used to make oil
7. a cold, sweet food that comes in many flavours
8. a long, yellow fruit that you have to peel

Exercise 2: Listen for Meaning

Listen to the information. Which of these topics did you hear about?

1. the origin of pasta
2. how to make spaghetti sauce
3. the kinds of milk that people drink
4. how people used watermelons in ancient Greece and Rome
5. how people used grapes in the past
6. when bananas first appeared in North America
7. the first person to taste a pineapple
8. how chocolate was first used

○ ○ Exercise 3: Listen for Details

Listen to the information. While you listen, answer the questions.

1. What country do most people associate with spaghetti or pasta?
2. What is pasta made of?
3. Where did pasta originate?
4. What was pasta made of originally?
5. Where did people first begin to milk farm animals?
6. What is the only form of milk that many Chinese people consume today?
7. Name some animals from which people get milk to drink.
8. Which animal has the richest milk on earth?
9. Explain how the ancient Greeks and Romans used watermelons.
10. Name three ways olive oil was used in the Mediterranean region.
11. How were bananas sold at the Centennial Exposition in Philadelphia?
12. Who was the first person in Europe to bite into a pineapple?
13. What happened when he bit into the pineapple? Why?
14. What was the original name for chocolate?
15. How was chocolate served in Europe?
16. What order did the king issue about chocolate?
17. What were plates made of, long ago?
18. What was considered bad manners?

Did You Know?   The ancient Romans drank milk only when it was mixed with wine.

Where Is the Kiwi From?

Complete the text with the correct words.

The kiwi is one of a small number of food plants that **1**_____ been
(have, was, is, has)
domesticated over the past thousand years. The original berry was known in

China in the eighth century, **2**_____ the kiwi fruit was domesticated in the
(and, but, so, if)
twentieth century in New Zealand. The first commercial orchard was established

on the northern island of New Zealand in 1937. From there, the fruit has gone on

to become an enormous commercial success **3**_____ the globe.
(around, of, under, in)
From relative obscurity in the 1930s, the kiwi fruit **4**_____ become a
(was, have, is, has)
popular food item in 30 countries. This amazing hairy berry is produced today in

the United States, France, Japan, Italy and 12 other countries.

5_____ the berry's widespread success, the main kiwi-
(Although, If, Despite, Since)
fruit producer is still New Zealand. In 1986 alone, one billion kiwi fruits were

exported from "down under." New Zealand's northern island is an ideal place to

grow kiwi fruit. They thrive in its warm, wet climate and volcanic soil. The egg-

sized brown berry we know today **6**_____ in the
(begun, originated, exported, gathered)
Yangtze Valley, where it grew wild in a smaller form. A traveller brought the first

kiwi to New Zealand in 1906 and over the years, it was developed into its

present size and taste.

Kiwi fruits taste good but they have another advantage. They preserve very

well. **7**_____ , at a temperature of 0°C, they
(However, Since, For example, Nevertheless)
will last in perfect condition for six months. They can also be stored for weeks in

a refrigerator at home. The green pulp inside **8**_____ its colour
(loses, retains, finds, sees)
even when exposed to air for long periods of time.

The berry was exported from New Zealand orchards to Europe only in the

1950s and to California in the 1960s. Its first success **9**_____ limited to
(had, was, has, have)

gourmet restaurants, but by the 1980s kiwis had become a staple in supermarkets in many countries. Kiwi-fruit farming has become **10**_____ extremely
(a, the, an, this)
important industry in New Zealand. Ten thousand people are employed annually to harvest kiwis. Millions of dollars are made **11**_____ kiwi farmers each year.
(into, of, from, by)
Even with competition from other producer countries, the New Zealand kiwi industry continues to hold a **12**_____ place in the world market. And the kiwi
(dominant, first, best, low)
fruit remains a source of wealth and pride for New Zealand.

Cookies

Today's cookies are crisp or chewy, and may contain raisins, chocolate chips, or nuts. If you had lived in Rome in the third century, however, your cookies would not have tasted as good. At that time, the cookie was thin and hard, and not very sweet. It was similar to a piece of dry bread. Sweet and tasty cookies did not become popular until the 1700s.

Fortune Cookies Debut in China

Exercise 1: Get Ready to Read

Discuss these questions in a group.

1. What are some symbols of good luck?

2. Do you ever cross your fingers, or carry a lucky charm, to ensure good luck?

3. What are some ways that people try to predict the future?

4. Do you know anyone who has had his or her fortune told? What happened?

Fortune Cookies Debut in China

Sheryl WuDunn

New York Times

HONG KONG—An old saying pokes fun at the eating habits of the southern Chinese: Whatever flies in the sky, whatever crawls on the ground, whatever swims in the sea, the Cantonese will eat it all. There is an exception, however, that may seem strange to North Americans. Very few Cantonese or Chinese elsewhere in Hong Kong, Taiwan or China have a taste for fortune cookies.

At Chinese restaurants across North America, fortune cookies usually go hand-in-hand with a Chinese meal. But many Chinese on the other side of the Pacific have never heard of fortune cookies, let alone eaten one.

Cater to foreigners

A year and a half ago, Nancy C. Anderson, a Chinese woman married to an American, tried to change this by introducing the cookie to Hong Kong. Now she imports fortune cookies made in California and sells them in Hong Kong to fancy delicatessens that cater to foreigners and young Chinese professionals. "Europeans and Americans here have this idea that fortune cookies come from China," says Anderson, 42, who was born in Shanghai. "They can't imagine they were made in the United States," she said.

Anderson advertises her product as "Genuine American Fortune Cookies." "Fortune cookies?" said a teacher in Beijing who lived in the United States for eight years. "Oh yes, I've seen them in the States."

The fortune cookie may have originally been created by Chinese immigrants in the United States, a makeshift rendition of a food or custom dear to them at home. Even Chinese restaurant owners in New York are puzzled by the origins of the fortune cookie, although they do say the cookie was a Chinese-American invention.

One version of the cookies' origin traces the notion of treats bearing messages back to the Yuan Dynasty in the 12th century. During the revolts against the Mongols, who had invaded and ruled China, rebel monks had devised a way to pass details about the rebellions to the peasants. So they slipped messages into mooncakes, a sweet holiday dessert, and sold them to the people.

Message-bearing cakes were also used in ancient Chinese parlour games. Players used to write wise and witty sayings on scraps of paper that were then inserted into twisted cakes. Anderson suspects Chinese immigrants remembered this bit of history when they settled in the United States.

Many of them were Buddhists, accustomed to going to temples to pray and have their fortunes told. Early Chinese immigrants had no temples for prayers and fortune-telling, Anderson said. So perhaps they baked mooncakes with fortunes in them and sold them in their restaurants, she said.

Another story traces the invention to George Jung, who founded the Hong Kong Noodle Co. in 1916 in Los Angeles. In her book, *Madame Chu's Chinese Cooking School,* Grace Zia Chu says that perhaps Jung created the fortune cookies to cheer people up after the First World War. But she also adds that Jung may have invented fortune cookies to amuse dinner guests while they waited for their orders.

Importing the cookie has forced Anderson and her Japanese suppliers in America to make a few changes in the way a fortune cookie is sold. Her cookies are individually wrapped in clear cellophane to protect against humidity and dirt during the long ocean voyage. To North Americans who are used to seeing a bunch of fortune cookies on a plate at the end of dinner, this may seem a little awkward, like single-wrapped Oreos.

Reverse habit

The Chinese also take a different approach to the cookie, trying to pluck out the fortune without letting the cookie crumble. Anderson then explained to them that it is proper to break the cookie to get the fortune. "The Chinese eat the cookie first and then look at the piece of paper," said Anderson. "Most Americans look at the fortune first."

In test marketing, Anderson was snubbed by many Chinese who had been to the United States and were used to receiving the cookies free after a Chinese meal. So Anderson has tried to sell to young Chinese professionals, who tend to read English and believe the cookie has a foreign cachet.

Her cookies have also been distributed by the Hong Kong government in a campaign against drugs. The messages had a fortune on one side and an anti-drug slogan on the other.

📖 Exercise 3: Read Carefully for Details

Work with a partner. Look in the text for the answers.

1. What have other Chinese sometimes said about the people of southern China?

2. When do people in North America eat fortune cookies?

3. Who is Nancy Anderson and what is her business?

4. Who eats fortune cookies in Hong Kong?

5. How did the teacher in Beijing know about fortune cookies?

6. Name two situations in which "message-bearing cakes" were used historically in China.

7. What connection is there between Buddhist traditions and fortune cookies?

8. Explain the two theories Madame Chu has about George Jung and fortune cookies.

9. What change has Anderson made in her fortune cookies?

10. Why would Americans find this change strange?

11. Compare Chinese and American ways of eating the cookies.

12. Why do many Hong Kong Chinese not like to buy Anderson's cookies?

13. In what way has the Hong Kong government used fortune cookies?

Exercise 4: Review Vocabulary

Match the columns to find words or expressions that have the same meaning.

1.	poke fun at	several
2.	hand-in-hand	together
3.	cater to	the idea
4.	puzzled	clever
5.	the notion	confused
6.	devise	laugh at
7.	witty	was ignored
8.	a bunch	supply
9.	to pluck out	invent
10.	was snubbed	to remove

How Do You Eat It?

Here are some foods that come from different places. Work in a group. Explain how you would eat any of the foods that are familiar to you.

1. couscous
2. a mango
3. an apple
4. pizza
5. kiwi
6. oysters
7. café au lait
8. a hamburger
9. crab
10. spaghetti
11. soup
12. shish kebab

The Kingdom of Plants: How Plants Are Used

Video Activity 1

Exercise 1: Get Ready to Watch the Video

What do you know about plants and the products we get from them? Do this quiz and find out. Work in a group. Choose the best answers.

1. Spruce trees grow in:

    a) swamps

    b) tropical rain forests

    c) northern forests

2. What happens first to logs at the sawmill?

    a) the rough bark is stripped off

    b) the trunks are cut into planks

    c) the trunks are cut into smaller logs

3. Wood pulp is used to make:

    a) matches

    b) paper

    c) flooring

4. Wheat has been cultivated for:

    a) 700 years

    b) 2100 years

    c) 9000 years

5. Wheat is harvested in:

    a) spring

    b) summer

    c) fall

6. Which foods are eaten by the most people?

    a) vegetables

    b) fruits

    c) seeds from plants

7. Where is rice not a part of the daily diet?

    a) India

    b) Sweden

    c) China

Did You Know?   A man in Edmonton has found a way to serve food in edible containers. Professor Buncha Ooraikul has invented special containers for yogurt, chili, coffee, hamburgers or french fries. When you finish eating, you just break off a piece of the plate, bowl or cup and continue eating. What a tasty way to save the environment from the effects of Styrofoam!

8. Coffee beans grow on:

   a) bushes

   b) trees

   c) the ground

9. What happens to coffee beans first?

   a) the beans are removed from the husks

   b) the beans are dried in the sun

   c) the beans are roasted and ground

10. The seeds of the cacao plant ripen in:

    a) baskets

    b) the grass

    c) banana leaves

11. Cacao is an important crop in:

    a) West Africa

    b) Canada

    c) Eastern Europe

12. The main ingredient for liquid chocolate is:

    a) cacao butter

    b) sugar cane

    c) milk

13. Sugar cane plants are set on fire to:

    a) kill insects

    b) solidify the liquid sugar

    c) burn off the leaves

14. Marmalade contains sugar and:

    a) oranges

    b) peaches

    c) grapes

15. Cotton is picked:

    a) by tractor

    b) by harvester

    c) by hand

16. Miners work underground to look for:

    a) coal

    b) oil

    c) wood

17. Coal is used:

    a) to produce electricity

    b) to feed people

    c) to power cars

18. Coal and gasoline come from:

    a) dead plants

    b) rocks

    c) earth

19. Lavender flowers and rose petals are used for:

    a) perfume

    b) medicine

    c) cooking

20. How many of our medicines today come from plants?

    a) most

    b) many

    c) a few

21. Some people use herbal remedies to treat:

    a) common illnesses

    b) severe illnesses

    c) unusual illnesses

22. If the rain forest is cut down, we will lose:

    a) good farm land

    b) tourist development areas

    c) plants that may contain medicines

Exercise 2: Watch the Video For Details

Watch the video. As you watch, look for the answers to the quiz in Exercise 1.

Food Customs

Exercise 1: Prepare a Report

Prepare a report on a traditional meal that you have in your family. The meal can be for a holiday, an anniversary, or any time family members traditionally get together. Plan to speak for about 15 minutes.

Exercise 2: Present

Present an oral report to the class or to your group. Give people a chance to ask you questions.

Exercise 3: Write

Write a summary of the information you gave in your report.

Unit 3

Welcome to Canada

The Great Canadian Quiz
Interaction
Cultural Information

Where Canadians Come From
Number Dictation
Cultural Information

Entering Canada
Listening Activity 3

Castor Canadensis
Vocabulary
Information Transfer

A Vast Country
Information Exchange

The Hudson's Bay Company
Reading
Cultural Information

About Canada
Writing

The Great Canadian Quiz

What do you know about Canada? Do this quiz to find out. Work in a group. Choose the best answers.

1. Where do nine out of ten Canadians live?
   a) in Ontario and Quebec
   b) in western Canada
   c) close to the United States border

2. How many time zones are there in Canada?
   a) three
   b) six
   c) nine

3. Which vegetable do Canadians eat most?
   a) corn
   b) the carrot
   c) the potato

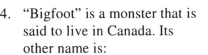

4. "Bigfoot" is a monster that is said to live in Canada. Its other name is:
   a) the Loch Ness Monster
   b) the Sasquatch
   c) Dracula

5. Which famous cheese was produced first in Ontario?
   a) cheddar
   b) mozzarella
   c) Parmesan

6. What information on an address identifies Canada's eighteen geographical regions?
   a) the street name
   b) the postal code
   c) the name of the province

7. Which is the largest island in Canada?
   a) Newfoundland
   b) Baffin Island
   c) Vancouver Island

8. If it is 10:00 a.m. in Ottawa, what time is it in Vancouver?
   a) 5:00 a.m.
   b) 7:00 a.m.
   c) 2:00 p.m.

9. What did Frederick G. Banting discover?
   a) how to fly a plane
   b) how to isolate insulin
   c) how to send radio signals

10. Which fruit does not grow in Canada?
    a) the grape
    b) the peach
    c) the orange

11. Where does Anne of Green Gables come from?
    a) New Brunswick
    b) Prince Edward Island
    c) Newfoundland

12. The world's biggest Easter Egg is in:
    a) Vegreville, Alberta
    b) Winnipeg, Manitoba
    c) Warsaw, Poland

13. What percentage of Canada's total area is farmland?
    a) 7 percent
    b) 27 percent
    c) 47 percent

14. What does CTV stand for?
    a) Canadian Tax Victims
    b) Canadian Television Network
    c) Canadian Transport Vehicles

15. Which is the highest Canadian waterfall?
    a) Takkakaw Falls
    b) Niagara Falls
    c) Angel Falls

16. This famous apple was first produced in Ontario.
    a) Golden Delicious
    b) McIntosh
    c) Spartan

17. Laura Secord became a famous figure in the War of 1812. Now "Laura Secord":
    a) is a coffee shop
    b) sells chocolates
    c) is a bakery

18. Which city has the biggest shopping mall?
    a) New York
    b) Edmonton
    c) Singapore

19. If someone in New Brunswick offered you a fiddlehead, what would you do?
    a) play music
    b) read it
    c) eat it

20. Which is the largest chartered bank in Canada?
    a) the Howard Bank
    b) the National Bank
    c) the Royal Bank

21. Canada's currency is regulated by:
    a) the Royal Canadian Mint
    b) the RCMP
    c) Canada Post

22. Which two famous soft drinks originated in Toronto?
    a) Canada Dry and Orange Crush
    b) Canada Dry and 7-Up
    c) Diet Pepsi and ginger ale

23. In the town of Dryden in Northern Ontario stands the world's biggest statue of:
    a) a penguin
    b) a moose
    c) a toucan

24. What are Bow Valley and Writing-on-Stone?
    a) Canadian rock groups
    b) provincial parks in Alberta
    c) grains grown in the prairies

Where Canadians Come From

As you listen, write the numbers in the spaces. Use the worksheet.

In 1970, most of the immigrants to Canada came from Britain. About _____
1
people came from Britain, which was slightly more than the _____ people who
2
came from the United States. Large numbers of immigrants came also from

Portugal (_____ people), Greece (_____ people), and India (_____ people).
3   4   5

In 1980, many immigrants arrived from different places. Vietnam provided

_____ people, Britain _____ people, and the United States _____ immigrants
6   7   8
to Canada. Hong Kong was next in line, with _____, slightly ahead of Laos,
9
which had _____. China followed with _____ people.
10   11

In 1990, Hong Kong led the way with _____ immigrants. Poland ranked
12
second, with _____, followed by Lebanon with _____ immigrants. At this
13   14
time, _____ arrived from the Philippines, and _____ from India. Vietnam
15   16
followed with _____ people. The number of immigrants from Portugal was
17
about _____; from China, _____; and from the United States, _____.
18   19   20

SIR CLIFFORD SIFTON

Did You Know? The world's first commercial motion picture was produced in Canada. In 1903 the minister responsible for immigration, Clifford Sifton, produced an advertising film aimed at attracting new farmers to the Canadian prairies.

Entering Canada

Listening Activity 3

Interview with Richard Goldman, Immigration Lawyer

Exercise 1: Get Ready to Listen

Discuss these questions in a group.

1. Why do people emigrate from their countries of birth? List as many reasons as you can.
2. Why do people immigrate to Canada?
3. In which parts of Canada do you think most immigrants settle?
4. Which people do you think are most likely to be admitted to Canada?
5. What kinds of questions do immigration officers ask potential immigrants?
6. Where can you get advice about immigration requirements?

Did You Know?	Between 1901 and 1919, the prairie provinces in the Canadian West saw very rapid growth. The population of Winnipeg grew from 42 000 to 200 000; Calgary went from 5000 to 75 000, and Edmonton grew from 2500 to 40 000. During the same time, the population of Vancouver on the Pacific coast rose from 27 000 to 123 000.

◯◯ **Exercise 2: Listen for Meaning**

Listen to the conversation. Then answer these questions with a partner.

1. What is the subject of the interview?
2. What are some topics that are covered in the interview?

◯◯ **Exercise 3: Listen for Details**

Listen to the conversation again. While you listen, answer the questions.

1. Where can a person apply if he or she wants to immigrate to Canada?
2. How long does it take for an application to be processed?
3. How many people is Canada presently accepting?
4. Who has the best chance of being accepted in Canada?
5. What other groups of people have a good chance of acceptance?
6. If someone from another country marries a Canadian, will he or she be automatically accepted into Canada?
7. What is a permanent resident?
8. What rights do permanent residents have?
9. Under what conditions can a person lose his or her permanent-resident status?
10. What does a landed immigrant have to do to become a Canadian citizen?
11. On what basis would a person be excluded from immigrating to Canada?
12. If a person is born in Canada, but lives elsewhere, is he or she a Canadian citizen?
13. Does Canada have a policy of dual citizenship?
14. Under what conditions does Canada accept a refugee?
15. How can a person obtain refugee status?

Did You Know?   The beaver appeared on the first Canadian postage stamp which was issued in 1851. The beaver appeared on the Canadian five-cent piece in 1937.

The scientific name for the beaver is *Castor Canadensis. Castor* is the Latin word for the beaver. *Canadensis* refers to Canada as the beaver's home.

Castor Canadensis

Exercise 1: Get Ready

☐☐ Choose the correct word for each space.

Castor Canadensis

Beavers are furry animals with wide, flat tails **1**_____ like
(made, shaped, look, seem)
paddles. They are well known for their skill at **2**_____ down
(falling, biting, cutting, eating)
trees with their large front teeth. They eat the bark, and use the tree trunks and

3_____ to build their dams and homes, which are called
(branches, flowers, plants, sticks)
lodges. Beavers always seem to be busy, and for this reason we often call a

hard worker "an eager beaver," or say that **4**_____ who
(those, someone, person, animal)
is working hard is "busy as a beaver."

Did you know that today's beaver is tiny compared with beavers long ago?

About 10 000 years ago, giant beavers grew to the size of black bears!

Beavers live in families in the ponds, **5**_____ , and
(cities, oceans, rivers, country)
streams of Canada. Beavers are excellent swimmers and divers. They build

dams made of sticks, stones, trees and mud. The **6**_____
(small, human, big, whole)
family works on the dam, and sometimes other beavers join in as well. Then

they build the lodges in which they live. They enter their lodges through a door

located beneath the **7**_____ .
(land, tree, water, forest)

Beavers are about 90 to 100 centimetres long, and can weigh up to 43

kilograms. They usually **8**_____ for life, and have litters of two to
(marry, live, want, mate)
four young, called kits. The kits usually stay with their parents for two years

before leaving to start their own families. A beaver's life **9**_____
(span, work, place, long)
is between 10 and 24 years.

Beavers have been known to cut down trees over one and a half metres

in circumference for their construction work. Their habits of building

10_____ and storing food seem to be instinctive.
(paths, dams, apartments, ponds)

Sometimes the sound of running **11**_____ is enough to
(feet, moose, trees, water)

stimulate a beaver to build a dam!

Exercise 2: Transfer Information

☐ ☐   Name the parts of the beaver and its surroundings. Use information from the
text.

A Vast Country

Partner A

Exercise 1: Get Ready

Look at Map A. Work in a group and write the names of any provinces and territories you can recognize. Use the worksheet.

Canada: Map A

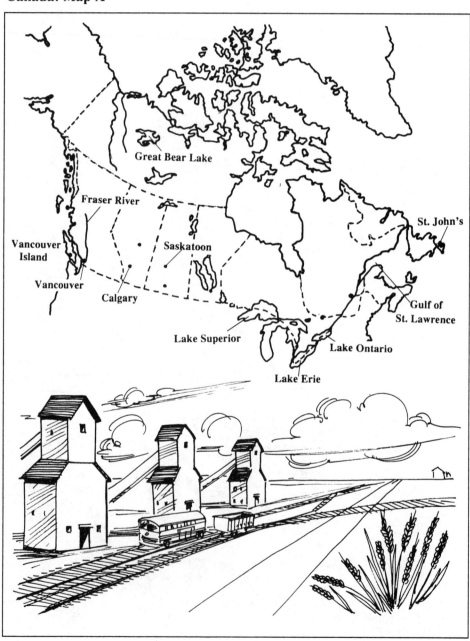

Exercise 2: Listen and Write

As the teacher gives the information, label the ten provinces and two territories. The information you hear will be similar to this:

> In the middle of Canada, near the Great Lakes, is the province of Ontario. Ontario touches Hudson Bay in the north and the United States border in the south. The capital of Ontario is Toronto. Please write "Ontario." O-N-T-A-R-I-O.

Exercise 3: Exchange Information

Work with a partner who has Map B. Ask your partner to give you information about the location of the following places and label them. Then give your partner information about places that you have on your map.

Baffin Island

Lake Huron

the McKenzie River

the Queen Charlotte Islands

Great Slave Lake

Victoria

Ottawa

Edmonton

Regina

Lake Winnipeg

Quebec City

A Vast Country

Partner B

Exercise 1: Get Ready

Look at Map B. Work in a group and write the names of any provinces and territories you can recognize. Use the worksheet.

Canada: Map B

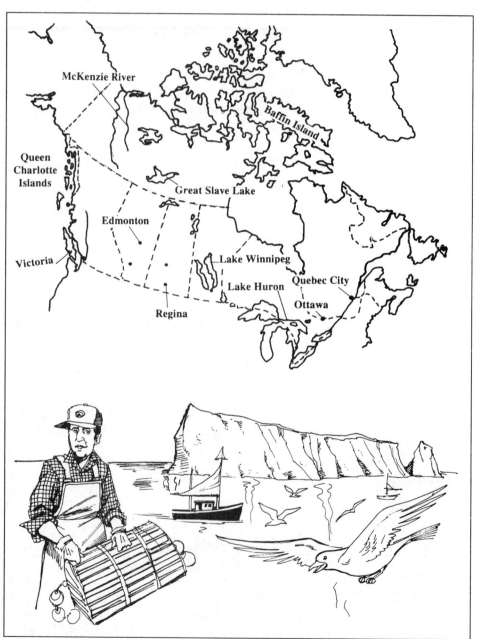

Exercise 2: Listen and Write

As the teacher gives the information, label the ten provinces and two territories. The information you hear will be similar to this:

In the middle of Canada, near the Great Lakes, is the province of Ontario. Ontario touches Hudson Bay in the north and the United States border in the south. The capital of Ontario is Toronto. Please write "Ontario." O-N-T-A-R-I-O.

Exercise 3: Exchange Information

☐☐ Work with a partner who has Map A. Give your partner information about the places you have on your map. Then ask your partner to exchange information by giving you the location of the following places:

Great Bear Lake	the Fraser River
Lake Ontario	the Gulf of St. Lawrence
Lake Superior	Vancouver Island
Lake Erie	Vancouver
Saskatoon	St. John's
Calgary	

The Hudson's Bay Company

Exercise 1: Get Ready to Read

☐☐ Do you like to shop? Do you know the names of the world's most famous department stores? Work with a partner to match the store to the city where it is located.

1.	Seibu	Moscow
2.	Sanborns	Toronto
3.	The Bay	Paris
4.	Galeries Lafayette	Mexico City
5.	Macy's	Tokyo
6.	Harrods	New York
7.	G.U.M.	Taiwan
8.	Makro	London
9.	Far East	Caracas

📖 Exercise 2: Read Quickly for General Ideas

Read the text quickly. Find the paragraphs that discuss the following:

1. the president's trials
2. why beaver fur was valuable
3. the Hudson's Bay Company today
4. the origins of the Hudson's Bay Company
5. the power of the Hudson's Bay Company at its height
6. dishonest practices

The Hudson's Bay Company

A. The Hudson's Bay Company is the oldest continuous trading company in the world. It has been in business for nearly 325 years. The history of the Hudson's Bay Company begins in 1670 when it was given a Royal Charter by the king of England. The charter entitled the company to exclusive fur-trading rights in the area of all rivers or streams that drained into Hudson Bay. This made the HBC the largest landholder of all time. Eventually the Hudson's Bay Company empire stretched across the North American continent to the Pacific Ocean and north to the Arctic Ocean. The Company's business was fur trading, and its history is part of the history of Canada.

B. The most valued items for the fur trade were beaver pelts. Before the invention of the umbrella, men in Europe used beaver-felt hats to keep their heads dry when it rained. Beaver hats were more than practical, however. They were very highly valued, and many traditions were associated with them. For example, beaver hats were passed down in families from father to son. They were also the basis of an enormously popular fashion trend. Throughout the eighteenth and nineteenth centuries, the way a man wore his hat placed him in the social hierarchy. Rules of etiquette prescribed the exact angle at which to wear a hat and the exact sweep to be used when removing it. The way a man lifted his hat to a lady or to a business associate or social acquaintance had the power to compliment or to insult.

C. Because beaver pelts were so valuable, fraudulent practices developed around their commerce. Poor-quality skins were substituted for good-quality ones. Pelts were stored in damp basements where the humidity would increase their weight. If they weighed more, the price would be higher. The Hudson's Bay Company traders did everything they could to keep the flow of pelts coming. Company trading posts were kept as cold as possible so that fur trappers wouldn't hang around the fire and miss chances to trap more beaver!

D. At its height, the Hudson's Bay Company was so powerful that it had its own money. The company had 178 trading posts and many agents who became legendary for their application, efficiency, and determination. Many items were traded to the Native peoples in exchange for beaver pelts. These included knives, axes and guns, copper cooking kettles, and the famous Hudson's Bay blankets. Unfortunately, brandy was also traded, introducing long-lasting problems across Native territories.

E. By 1859, the fur trade had begun to slow down and the Company sold all but three million hectares of its land to the Government of Canada for a price of 300 000 pounds. Today, the Hudson's Bay Company has stopped trading in beaver fur and is primarily a department store chain with some interests in real estate. For the HBC, the fur trade is over. For the beaver, however, it may not be. One might wonder how the Canadian beaver feels about the HBC, its once formidable enemy. One might wonder whether the rodent might not want revenge for those terrible years of being hunted to satisfy the fashion trends of Europe.

F. A recent event lends support to this fanciful theory. The current president of the Hudson's Bay Company has a country house outside Toronto. One day, the president woke up to find that some trees on his property had been cut down during the night. When he went to investigate, he was horrified to find tooth marks at the base of the trees. To protect his property, he put steel plates around the bases of the trees. When this failed, he tried making noise to scare the beavers away. He even used TNT to blow up their dams. But Canadian beavers, like the HBC agents, are legendary for their application, efficiency, and determination. At last report, the president's trees were still crashing down around the property. Perhaps it is fitting that the beavers, who needed logs for their homes, had come to the property of the president of the HBC!

Exercise 3: Read Carefully for Details

Work with a partner. Look in the text for the answers.

1. What kind of record does the Hudson's Bay Company hold?
2. How extensive was the Hudson's Bay Company's empire?
3. How were beaver pelts used?
4. What tradition was associated with beaver-felt hats?
5. Give examples of rules for wearing the beaver-felt hat in social situations.
6. Name two dishonest practices associated with beaver pelts.
7. Why were HBC trading posts so cold?
8. Give evidence of the power of the Hudson's Bay Company.
9. Describe the characteristics of the agents at the Hudson's Bay Company.
10. What were some items that the Company traded for beaver pelts?
11. When did the fur trade slow down?
12. What is the HBC's business today?
13. What fanciful theory is referred to?
14. What did the president of the HBC find at the base of his trees?
15. How did he try to discourage the beavers?
16. Why was it fitting that the beavers were cutting trees on the property of the president of the HBC?

Exercise 4: Review Vocabulary

☐☐ Find the words in the text with the same meaning as the words or expressions below.

Paragraph A:	biggest	extended
Paragraph B:	prized	fad
Paragraph C:	dishonest	exchanged
Paragraph D:	skins	enduring
Paragraph E:	mainly	terrifying
Paragraph F:	imaginary	appropriate

About Canada

Write about the way you feel about living in Canada.

Did You Know? In the seventeenth century, beavers were so famous for their industry and engineering skills that people in Europe used to imagine them living in multi-storey houses in the Canadian forests!

Unit 4

Safe and Sound

Safety Mistakes

Exercise 1: Get Ready

Work with a partner. Look at the picture. How many safety mistakes can you find?

Exercise 2: Read and Discuss

Read these paragraphs. Discuss the safety mistakes. List some actions that can be taken to prevent these emergency situations in the future.

1. One morning at 5:00 a.m. Helen B. woke up to feed her infant. As she arose, she smelled smoke. She quickly woke her husband and discovered that the hall was filled with smoke. The couple snatched up their baby, ran out of the house and called the fire department from a neighbour's home. After the fire department had the fire under control, they discovered that some clothing stored on the top shelf of a closet had fallen against a light bulb. The closet light had been left on, and the clothes had begun to burn. At the bottom of the closet, still in their original box, were two smoke detectors.

2. Talking on the telephone during an electric storm almost cost James F. his life. He had just hung up the phone after a long conversation with a friend when lightning hit a telephone pole next to his house. The lightning surged through the wires, knocking the telephone right off the wall.

3. One bitterly cold winter morning in January, as Lea G. was driving to work, she noticed a small boy sitting on the curb, crying. It seemed he had missed his school bus. No one was at home, and he had no key for his house. He also had no money, and didn't know his parents' number at work.

4. Janet Y. had heard about the proper techniques for helping a tired swimmer, but she had never needed to use them. One day at the lake, she noticed that an elderly man who was swimming near her was becoming tired. As he became more and more out of breath, he became frightened. Janet persuaded him to hang on to her shoulder as she swam to shore. She was very fortunate that this action did not cost her her life.

5. Nick P. was frying potatoes to make french fries, when the grease in the pan suddenly burst into flames. He threw the pan into the sink, and turned on the water. Amazingly, the fire did go out, but grease was spattered everywhere. He was extremely fortunate that the curtains above the sink didn't catch fire. Had he used the proper techniques, he would have avoided that danger.

6. Nancy M. was babysitting for her neighbour's three-year-old daughter. She took the little girl to the park, where there was a wading pool for children. At the park, Nancy met her friend. As Nancy and her friend chatted, she noticed that the little girl was playing near the edge of the pool, but she didn't notice when the child began to inch her way along the pool's edge. Then, as the little girl reached for a leaf, she fell head-first into the water. Luckily, a woman saw the child and pulled her out.

Fire Safety: How to Survive

Exercise 1: Get Ready to Read

Work in a group. Discuss each statement and decide if it is true (**T**) or false (**F**).

1. Most people don't have any experience dealing with a fire.
2. If a fire breaks out in a wastebasket, you have a few minutes to think about what to do.
3. The heat from a fire can kill you instantly.
4. Most people know instinctively what to do in a fire.
5. If you live in an apartment building and a fire breaks out, you should proceed quickly to the ground floor by elevator.
6. It is a good idea to close your bedroom door every night, in case of fire.
7. The best way to reach the exit is to run through the smoke quickly.
8. The freshest air is near the floor.
9. One smoke alarm in your house or apartment is enough.
10. It is recommended that you put a fire extinguisher next to your stove in the kitchen.
11. One fire extinguisher will suit all purposes.
12. Carefully checking dangerous areas of your house will reduce the risk of fire.

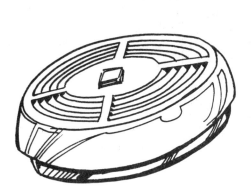

Exercise 2: Read Quickly to Check Predictions

Read the text quickly. Find the answers to the true/false questions in Exercise 1.

Fire Safety: How to Survive

C.D. Clark

Info Club, *Club Price News*

It could be the most important meeting you ever have. In the event of a fire, it could save your life or your child's.

Take an hour or two this week to map out escape routes from your home, install proper smoke or fire detectors, and learn where danger lurks in your home. If you've already done these things, take half an hour to review the escape route (it may need updating) and to check the batteries in your smoke detectors. You trust your life to these devices every time you go to bed, so make sure they're working.

Few people ever have to escape from a burning building, so when it happens it is likely to be the first time. You will be surprised by how the smoke blocks out all light; you will be shocked by the difficulty of breathing, and you won't be able to detect the carbon monoxide gas, an invisible, odourless killer. You won't believe how little time you have to react. A tiny wastebasket fire can consume a house in two minutes. And you won't realize until it's too late that the heat from a fire can kill you instantly if you panic and open a door without feeling for heat on the other side. At 65°C, your body stops working. You are no match for a sofa that's been burning for only one minute; it can reach a temperature of 371°C.

The Plan

No one instinctively knows what to do in the face of an inferno. You need a plan.

First of all, draw a floor plan of your home, apartment or business. Show all possible exits from all rooms and know at least two ways out of every room, including windows if there is only one door and you can get to ground level safely. If you live on the second or third floor, you might want to get a safety ladder.

High-rise dwellers should learn all possible routes to stairwells. Learn the layout of your floor and of the ones above and below you. They may become part of your escape route. Most importantly, never use an elevator to escape a fire, no matter how safe it appears to be at the time. Fire can damage the controls, stranding you with no possible escape.

Once you've planned your escape routes, practise them with the whole family. Have everyone start in bed with the door closed. One person yells to simulate an alarm. Everyone touches his or her door. Pretend it is cool and exit that way; pretend it is hot and use the alternate route.

If the alarm sounds for real, remember:

• Closed doors slow fires, so close bedroom doors at night and close doors behind you as you escape.

• Roll out of bed and drop to the floor. (The cleanest and coolest air will be closest to the ground.) Crawl directly to the door and touch it.

• If the door is cool, open it a crack and check for smoke. If the hall is clear, crawl out and follow your escape route.

• If the door is hot, do not open it. Stop and think about your alternate route before taking it. You have a few seconds to collect your thoughts. You must assume that the rest of your family is following the same procedure, so dashing out and risking your life to check on them is not necessary.

• If you can't get out of the room or apartment, seal any cracks around doors and vents as best as you can, using wet towels if possible. Open a window and stay low beside it, breathing fresh air. If you can call the fire department, say precisely where you are in the building. Otherwise, shout for help and wave a brightly coloured garment to signal your position.

• If your clothes catch fire, stop, drop to the ground and roll. Do not run: that will only increase the flames.

• Teach small children never to hide under their beds.

• Meet outside at a predetermined point and take a head count. Do not go back into the building. It is important that you be able to tell the fire-fighters exactly who is missing and where the person is likely to be in the house.

Smoke Alarms

Your plan isn't any good if you don't have a functioning smoke detector to alert you to the danger. Manufacturers of smoke alarms, extinguishers and other safety products offer several tips about where to locate alarms and extinguishers.

Alarms should be placed in hallways between nearby bedrooms, or outside every bedroom if they are spread out through the house. They should also be installed inside every smoker's bedroom and in every room with an electrical appliance. There should be alarms on every floor of your house, including the attic if it is furnished. Basement alarms should be placed at the bottom of the stairwell. Second floor alarms should be installed at the top of the stairwell coming up from the first floor.

Experts also recommend having a fire extinguisher on each floor. It is especially important to have one in the kitchen, but it should not be too close to the stove. You might also consider one for your car. In all cases, the unit should be placed just inside the door of the room, easy to get at but close to the escape route so you can get out if the blaze cannot be controlled. Extinguishers are rated for different purposes, so read the specs before purchasing and check the pressure gauge monthly.

Danger Spots

While you are placing smoke detectors and drawing your floor plan, take note of particularly dangerous areas in your home.

Careful attention to these spots reduces the risk of fire.

Bedroom: do not smoke in bed, make sure all windows open and never put another blanket on top of an electric blanket.

Living room: use proper size bulbs in lights, replace frayed cords and loose switches and avoid running cords under rugs. Keep floor heaters three feet away from drapes and other flammable items.

Kitchen: frayed cords are dangerous here too. So is loose clothing when you are working around the stove. Use the pot lid to smother pot fires: do not use water. And buy appliances that shut off automatically if left unattended.

Exercise 3: Read Carefully for Details

Work with a partner. Look in the text for the answers.

1. Why is it important to have an escape plan?
2. Name three things that surprise people when they are in a burning building.
3. How fast can a wastebasket fire burn a house?
4. How fast can the heat from a fire kill a person?
5. At what temperature does your body stop working?
6. How high a temperature can a burning sofa reach in one minute?
7. Why do you need a plan in case of a fire?
8. What should your floor plan show?
9. What two things should apartment dwellers learn?
10. Why should you not use an elevator in case of fire?
11. Describe how you can practise your escape route with your family.
12. Why is it important to close doors?
13. What should you do if you are in bed and a fire starts?
14. What should you do if the hall is clear?
15. What should you do if the door is hot?
16. What can you do if you can't get out of your room?
17. What should you do if your clothes catch fire?
18. How should you arrange to meet other family members?
19. Where should fire alarms be placed?
20. How many alarms should you have?
21. Where should fire extinguishers be placed?
22. What should be done to avoid starting fires in the bedroom?
23. Where should floor heaters be placed in the living room?
24. How should you smother fires in a pot?

Accidents and Injuries

Exercise 1: Get Ready

Most people consider the home to be a safe place, but it might be the most dangerous place of all. About one third of all accidents occur in the home. Other common places where accidents take place are on roads and highways, in the workplace, and in public places. It is reassuring to know, however, that nearly all accidents can be prevented by following basic safety rules. Knowing what to do can help save lives.

Exercise 2: Discuss

Do you know what to do in an emergency? Do this quiz to find out. Work in a group. Choose the best answers.

1. To treat a burn:
   a) apply butter or a greasy substance
   b) immerse burned area in cool water
   c) immerse burned area in warm water

2. If someone starts to choke, you should:
   a) slap him or her on the back
   b) encourage him or her to talk
   c) encourage him or her to cough

3. The symptoms of frostnip (frostbite) are:
   a) skin irritation
   b) a white patch of skin
   c) a red patch of skin

4. Which of these could not be symptoms of a heart attack?
   a) pain in chest, neck, or shoulders
   b) weakness, nausea, shortness of breath
   c) coughing, sneezing, high fever

5. If someone is poisoned, you should give him or her:
   a) medication
   b) food
   c) water

6. The treatment for frostbite is:
   a) warm the area with a warm hand
   b) rub the area vigorously
   c) apply heat to the area

7. Someone's airway is completely obstructed if the person:
   a) is unable to speak or breathe
   b) cannot move
   c) is red in the face

8. If a person's clothing catches on fire:
   a) roll the victim in a coat or blanket
   b) use a fire extinguisher
   c) tell the victim to run

9. The Heimlich manoeuvre is:
   a) a new dance for teenagers
   b) a treatment for choking
   c) a method to help someone sober up

10. The parts of the body most susceptible to frostbite are:
    a) the legs
    b) the nose and cheeks
    c) the top of the head

Exercise 3: Read for Information

Read the information from the Red Cross safety card to check your answers.

BURNS

Tissue injuries resulting from over-exposure to excessive heat. Possible sources of heat include: thermal, chemical, electrical or radiation source (sun).

Types of burns
1st degree burn: redness. This is a very minor burn, but can be very painful.
2nd degree burn: redness and formation of blisters.
3rd degree burn: charred-blackened appearance.

First Aid for burns
1st degree: Immerse the burned area in cool water at once.
2nd degree: Immerse the burned area in cool water at once. Do not break blisters.
3rd degree: Cover the entire burn lightly with a lint-free cloth.
Seek medical attention immediately.

Important notice
- Do not apply butter or other greasy substance to a burn.
- For eye burns caused by chemical splash, flush the eye(s) with large amounts of water for at least 10 minutes, including under eye lids from the inside to the outside. Ensure the drainage from the burned eye does not run into the other eye.
- If clothing catches on fire:
  - restrain the victim from running;
  - do not use a fire extinguisher;
  - lie the victim on the ground;
  - ask the victim to cover his/her face with the hands; and
  - roll the victim in a blanket or large coat to smother the fire.

LIFE IS OUR CONCERN.

POISONING

When to suspect it:
- Any victim found unconscious, confused, or suddenly ill with suspected access to poisonous substance (usually children).
- Odor of poison on breath.
- Visible burns around the mouth.
- Open medicine or chemicals found in the presence of the victim.
- Sudden burning or pain in the throat.

Do...
1. Immediately obtain medical assistance: hospital emergency room, Poison Centre, doctor, or family physician.
2. Poison Centre phone number: (_____) _____.
3. If no medical assistance is available and if the victim is conscious, dilute poison by administering a non-toxic liquid (preferably water).
4. Keep airway open.
5. If victim vomits, turn victim on his or her side and retain sample.
6. Start rescue breathing and/or cardiopulmonary resuscitation if necessary.
7. Bring container of poison to hospital and have it on hand when calling the Poison Centre.

Do not...
1. Give fluids to unconscious victim.
2. Give ipecac or any other medication unless instructed to do so by medical personnel.

RED CROSS IS CONCERNED WITH YOUR SAFETY.

HEART ATTACK

When to suspect it:
Any victim who develops pain in the chest that may radiate to arms, shoulders, neck or jaw. Victim usually gets very weak, nauseated, and short of breath. Victim may perspire.

Do...
1. Seek medical assistance immediately, preferably without leaving the victim.
2. Place casualty in a comfortable position.
3. Assist the casualty in taking medication if a prescription is at hand.
4. Constantly check for victim's breathing and pulse.
5. Ensure the casualty has a clear airway.
6. Start rescue breathing and/or cardiopulmonary resuscitation if necessary.
7. Have victim examined by medical personnel even if victim appears to recover.

Do not...
Leave victim unattended unless absolutely necessary.

AIRWAY OBSTRUCTION

1. Partial obstruction
Signs:
• Able to inhale some air.
• Coughs forcefully.
Treatment:
• Encourage casualty to cough.
• Do not stop casualty's attempts to free own airway.

2. Complete obstruction
Signs:

• High-pitched or crowing-like noises.
• Unable to breathe or speak.
• Clutches at throat, begins turning blue.
• Increasing weakness.
Treatment:
• Call for help.
• Apply Heimlich maneuver:
  - go behind the person, place your arms around her waist;
  - form a fist with one hand, place it thumb-side in, against the victim's abdomen in midline slightly above the navel;
  - grasp the fist with the other hand; and
  - press the fist into the victim's abdomen with a quick upward thrust.
• Repeat above sequence until the victim breathes again.

FIRST AID MEANS BEING READY TO ACT IN EMERGENCY.

FROSTNIP

Frostnip is a superficial injury caused by freezing of a small area such as the nose, cheek, fingers or toes.

Symptoms:
• Possible pain or stinging in the frostnipped area followed by numbness.
• Area may appear whiter than the surrounding tissue.

Do...
1. Warm the area by steady firm pressure with a warm hand.
2. Blow hot breath on the area.
3. Hold frostnipped area such as fingers against the body (i.e. in armpits).

Do not...
1. Rub frostnipped area.
2. Expose areas to high temperatures.
3. Disturb blisters.

Your gift + is life!

A GIFT OF BLOOD IS A GIFT OF LIFE.

Medical Emergencies

Listening Activity 4

Interview with Dr. Debra Finestone

Exercise 1: Get Ready to Listen

Discuss these questions in a group.

1. In Canada, in what situations should you go to an emergency ward? In what situations should you go to your doctor?

2. Have you even been to an emergency ward in Canada or in another country? Explain what happened.

3. How are emergency wards in Canada similar to, or different from, those in other countries?

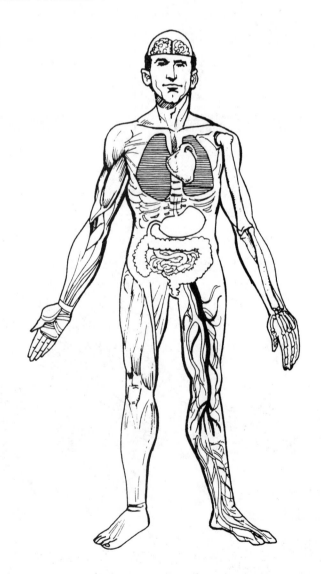

Exercise 2: Listen for Meaning

Listen to the interview. Which of these topics are discussed?

1. reasons why people go to the emergency ward
2. examples of rare diseases that must be seen by a doctor
3. causes of injuries to children around the home
4. the procedure that you can expect in an emergency ward
5. information on how to call an ambulance
6. what to do if you have a severe headache
7. what to do if you need further medical care

Exercise 3: Listen for Information

Listen to the conversation. While you listen, answer the questions.

1. What are two main reasons for going to the emergency ward of a hospital?
2. Give some examples of common injuries.
3. Give examples of common illnesses that bring people to the emergency ward.
4. What are some accidents that can occur in the kitchen?
5. Why do people often fall in the bathroom?
6. Give two reasons why elderly people often fall at home.
7. What kind of leg or foot injury should be seen at the hospital?
8. When is a high fever particularly worrisome?
9. When you arrive in emergency, who will see you first?
10. What does a triage nurse do?
11. What will a doctor do if you need follow-up after an emergency-room visit?
12. What will happen if you don't have a family physician?
13. What will happen if there is no 24-hour pharmacy in your area?

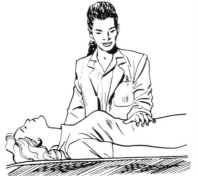

Exercise 4: Review Vocabulary

☐☐   Work with a partner. Find the following:

stretcher   wheelchair   walker   sling   crutch   cane
I.V. (intravenous)   nurse   paramedic   cast

Frozen Stiff

Exercise 1: Get Ready to Read

Discuss these questions in a group.

1. How cold can it get during the winter in Canada?

2. What can you do to protect yourself from the cold?

3. In what circumstances could someone get caught outside without shelter?

4. What would happen if a person were caught outside without shelter during the winter?

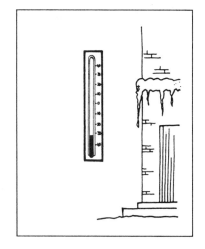

Exercise 2: Read to Increase Speed

Work with a partner. Read three paragraphs. Then stop and tell each other what you can remember.

Frozen Stiff

A. Late one night in December of 1992, Tanya Cooper was driving to visit her parents at their farmhouse near Wawa, Ontario. The young architect had been driving for hours since leaving her home in Toronto, and she was getting tired. As she rounded a bend in the road, she suddenly felt the car begin to slide. She struggled to regain control of the automobile.

B. In winter, the roads of northern Ontario are covered with ice, making it easy to lose control of a car in a turn at high speed. Cooper's car had hit a patch of ice and was out of control. The car skidded off the road, nearly hitting a tree, and landed in a large snowbank by the side of the road. Although the snow bank allowed Cooper to survive the crash without injury, her car was trapped in the snow and could not be moved without a tow truck.

C. Cooper waited in the car with the heater on, until she remembered that leaving a car with the engine running for a long time can cause the car to fill up with carbon monoxide and poison the occupants. She decided that she would rather be cold than dead. After waiting a long time for someone to drive down the deserted road, Cooper decided to get out and begin the 4-kilometre walk to the nearest farmhouse. She was wearing only a basic winter coat and light city boots, and she soon began to feel very cold in the minus 23° weather. As she trudged through the snow, Cooper kept hoping she would hear the sound of a car coming. No traffic seemed to be on the road that night.

D. As she continued on through the night, she felt colder and colder and began to feel extremely tired. It was difficult for her to keep walking. Each step was a tremendous effort. Then she saw a farmhouse off the road just ahead. Cooper staggered toward it, but approximately 20 metres from the house, she collapsed in the snow.

E. Cases such as Cooper's are not uncommon. Many drivers leave their cars when the vehicles become disabled in winter. Some of them, like Tanya Cooper, become victims of hypothermia, a condition that can occur in cold temperatures. Hypothermia sets in when the temperature of the body becomes very low, and internal organs respond by slowing their activity. The body needs less oxygen to continue operating if activity slows in this way. In a state of hypothermia, the heart rate and respiration become so slow that people are often mistaken for dead.

F. Nearly six hours after Cooper collapsed, Ray Pinto was on his way out of the farmhouse to begin his morning chores. He discovered Cooper, lying unconscious in the snow. Mr. Pinto shouted to his wife to come and help him take the young woman to the hospital. To their dismay, they discovered that they couldn't get her into the car because her joints were frozen stiff. In desperation they decided to wrap her in warm blankets and load her into the back of their pickup truck. Afraid that she might be dead, they rushed her to the hospital, praying they weren't too late.

G. At Wawa General Hospital, doctors found Cooper's body temperature too low for their thermometers to measure. Thermometers are designed to measure temperatures as low as 31°C. Only a faint heartbeat told the medical staff that she was alive. The doctors wanted to give Cooper an intravenous solution to replace her body's electrolytes but their needles could not pierce her skin. They tried to lower her into a warm bath but she was as stiff as a board. They eventually used warm sponges to thaw her out. Finally they were able to locate a vein and give her the intravenous solution.

H. The physician who treated Cooper explained: "Usually brain cells start to die after 3 or 4 minutes without blood flow. When this happens, permanent damage occurs. Hypothermia has the effect of slowing down the brain's activity to such a degree that it is in a state of suspended animation. This is what allowed Tanya Cooper to survive much longer than 4 minutes, without brain damage. You see, when hypothermia sets in, the cells are protected. Everything is slowed down. Because tissues are doing less, they require less oxygen to survive. It's very similar to what animals do when they hibernate in winter."

I. Miraculously, Tanya Cooper survived her ordeal without brain damage. Her skin was damaged by frostbite, which required medical treatment, but otherwise she came through a terrible experience with almost no after-effects. Cooper's terrifying experience has helped to focus attention on hypothermia as an emerging medical problem.

J. Once thought to be a rare occurrence, hypothermia is now viewed by doctors as a major unrecognized danger. There are two types of hypothermia: primary, which develops from long-term exposure to very cold temperatures— as in Tanya Cooper's case; and secondary, which is caused by an abnormality in the brain's thermostat. Secondary hypothermia can be caused by several factors: the body's decreased ability to maintain normal temperatures as a person ages, or drugs that lower the body temperature to a dangerously low level.

K. The second type of hypothermia is the most dangerous, because few people recognize the symptoms. Symptoms may be provoked by prescription or over-the-counter medications, alcohol, or a combination of alcohol and drugs. Some medications such as antidepressants, tranquillizers, or cough syrup can chemically lower the body's internal thermostat to produce potentially fatal hypothermia. This can occur even without freezing temperatures. Given the right conditions, even relatively moderate room temperatures can play a part in drug-induced hypothermia. Studies have shown that these types of cases are surprisingly frequent, even during relatively mild winters. Elderly people are particularly vulnerable, as they try to economize by keeping their home temperatures lower. Then, even commonly prescribed drugs can induce hypothermia, often with devastating results.

L. What can you do to protect yourself from hypothermia when travelling in cold weather? Doctors and highway police recommend that people travelling by car in winter be prepared. Make sure you carry some warm clothing or blankets in the car. Have matches and flares that you can use to alert passing motorists if you are in trouble. Do not leave your car. Even if it is cold, it offers some protection against the freezing temperatures you may encounter outside.

Exercise 3: Read Carefully for Details

Work with a partner. Look in the text for the answers.

1. Where was Tanya Cooper travelling?
2. Why did her car go out of control?
3. Why was she not injured when the car skidded off the road?
4. Why did she turn off the heater in the car?
5. Why did she decide to leave the car?
6. Why was her clothing inappropriate in the circumstances?
7. Describe Cooper's progress as she walked away from her car.
8. What is hypothermia?
9. What is the benefit to internal organs when they slow their activity?
10. When did Ray Pinto find Tanya Cooper?
11. Why didn't they put her in their car?
12. How did they get her to the hospital?
13. What two problems did doctors have in treating Cooper at first?
14. How does hypothermia protect against brain damage?
15. What was Tanya Cooper's medical condition?
16. Describe two types of hypothermia.
17. What can cause the second type of hypothermia?
18. Give examples of conditions that can cause the second type of hypothermia.
19. Who is most susceptible to the second type of hypothermia? Why?
20. What do doctors and highway police recommend for people travelling by car in winter?

Exercise 4: Review Vocabulary

☐ ☐   Locate the words in the left-hand column in the text. Then match them to the words on the right.

1. rounded   stumbled

2. struggled   walked

3. skidded   unfreeze

4. occupants   breathing

5. trudged   fought

6. staggered   turned

7. collapsed   slid

8. respiration   weak

9. chores   fell down

10. dismay   caused

11. load   put

12. faint   passengers

13. thaw   tasks

14. hibernate   disappointment

15. ordeal   painful experience

16. provoked   sleep

Did You Know?   The discovery of the principle of hypothermia made open-heart surgery possible. This discovery was made by a Canadian doctor, Wilfred Bigelow.

Unit 5

The Job Market

On the Job, Off the Job

Exercise 1: Discuss

Discuss these questions in a group.

1. Have you ever had a job in the past?

2. What kind of work did you do?

3. How did you get the job?

4. If you work now, how did you get your job?

5. If you have never worked in Canada, how do you think people get jobs here?

6. Name five different jobs you would like to have.

7. Discuss why these jobs seem attractive to you.

8. Reach a consensus in your group. Rank the following factors according to which are most important in determining a good job. Number 1 is most important.

   a) job security

   b) status of the position

   c) interesting or challenging work

   d) a good salary

   e) paid vacations

   f) opportunities for travel

   g) possibilities for advancement

   h) social benefits (vacation pay, sick leave, parental leave, etc.)

   i) a good boss

Exercise 2: Review Vocabulary

Work with a partner. Match the expressions to their meanings.

1. a job opening — a list of your duties
2. to be laid off — a personnel officer (human resources)
3. to be hired — a person asking for a job
4. prior work history — a position that is available
5. job skills — letters from former employers
6. to get fired — jobs you have done in the past
7. references — tasks you are trained to do
8. a recruiter — to lose a job due to lack of work
9. an applicant — to get a job
10. a job description — to lose a job as a result of poor performance

The Job Search

Exercise 1: Get Ready to Read

Discuss these statements about looking for a job in Canada. Which things should you do and which should you not do?

Work in a group. Write "Do" or "Don't" for each statement.

1. Collect all your work-related documents in case you get called for an interview.
2. Spend time making a list of the kinds of jobs you would like to have.
3. Avoid wasting your time by applying to companies that don't have ads in the newspaper.

4. Save your energy by looking for one job at a time.
5. Go to the nearest Canada Employment Centre to get advice about job hunting, and check lists of jobs that are posted.
6. Check newspapers for advertisements that ask you to invest some money but suggest you will make your money back by working.
7. Rely on newspaper ads as the best way to find a job.
8. Tell other people that you are looking for a job.
9. Take a job temporarily while you are waiting for the exact job you want to come along.
10. Try to answer as many questions as possible on the phone if someone calls you for a job interview.

Exercise 2: Read Quickly to Check Predictions

Read the text and check your answers to the questions you have just discussed. In which line do you find each answer?

The Job Search

Looking for a job can be an exciting experience that offers new opportunities. However, job hunting can also be a frustrating and discouraging experience that leaves people feeling rejected and depressed. Almost everyone will have the experience of looking for a job at least a few times in his or her life, so it
5   is useful to know what you should and should not do to improve your chances of success. Employment counsellors suggest that having some good strategies can be an enormous help in finding a job.

It is important to begin a job search by collecting all the documents that may be needed when applying for a job. Depending on the job, the employer may
10   ask for educational diplomas, degrees, and certificates of competence. If original documents are not in either English or French, they should be translated by an official translator. Letters of reference and copies of the candidate's curriculum vitae are other useful papers to have at hand. The most important document a person needs when looking for work in Canada is the
15   social insurance card that shows the Social Insurance Number, or SIN, that prospective employers are required by law to demand. Canadian citizens and landed immigrants can apply for their cards at Canada Employment Centres.

Employment counsellors say that people who are likely to get jobs quickly share several characteristics. They are mature; they are realistic; and they
20   show initiative. Job hunting is a full-time occupation so you should get up early, organize your plans for the day, and dress for the job at hand. To begin your job search, make a list of the jobs you may be qualified to do. Then, scout out the market in your area. Use the yellow pages to get information about companies that might need someone with your qualifications. Apply
25   even if these companies are not advertising for help. Many companies have openings that are not advertised. Apply to as many places as possible to increase your chances of success. Don't count on the first job you apply for to come through.

Canada Employment Centres, which are operated by the federal government,
30   can be a good source of help. They have lists of job opportunities, both locally and in other parts of the country. Counsellors are available to help people improve their job-hunting skills and to give out information about training courses and language classes. The classified section of the newspaper can be useful too. Beware of ads that promise amazing opportunities with a
35   small investment, however. Ads like that often lead to people losing their money!

Although advertisements are useful, employment counsellors say that they are not the best source of jobs. They recommend networking, pointing out that between 40 and 70 percent of the jobs people get come from information

40 received through personal contacts. Counsellors advise telling your family, your relatives, old school friends, your dry-cleaner, and everyone else you know that you would like to find a job. They suggest that you mention in a pleasant voice that you are looking for work, and that you be direct and say, "Do you know of any jobs available in _____?"

45 Counsellors also recommend that job hunters be flexible. They warn against ruling out jobs that might be a second or third choice. If you get your foot in the door, other jobs may become available later. Temporary jobs often end up as permanent jobs too. Companies are more likely to offer permanent jobs to people they already know than to take a chance on an unknown.

50 An important aspect of the job search is interview skills. If a prospective employer calls, it is best to arrange for a face-to-face interview. An interview is the key to being hired, but the dynamics of every interview are different. Successful applicants are often the ones who are best prepared. It is a good idea to find out about the company or organization in advance. Having

55 background information will help the applicant focus the answers. First impressions are very important, so the candidate should be sure to dress neatly, arrive on time, and give a firm handshake. Then, eventually, the job search will be successful.

Exercise 3: Read Carefully for Details

1. What are some feelings people have when they are looking for jobs?

2. Which documents should you have ready when you are job hunting?

3. What is an SIN card? Where can you get one?

4. What characteristics do good job candidates have in common?

5. List three things you should do when you are job hunting.

6. What should you do when you begin your job search?

7. Where can you get information about companies in your area?

8. Why is it a good idea to apply for more than one job at a time?

9. What kind of help can you get at Canada Employment Centres?

10. Which section of the newspaper has information about jobs?

11. Why should you be careful about opportunities that ask you to invest money?

12. What is the best way to find a job?

13. Whom should you tell about your job search?

14. Why is it a good idea to take a job that is not your first choice?

15. What is the benefit of taking a temporary job?

16. What should you do if a prospective employer calls?

17. How can you prepare for a job interview?

18. What can you do to create a good first impression?

The Formal Application

Exercise 1: Get Ready

Almost everybody who has a job has gone through the process of making applications. Generally, people go through the process quite a few times before they find a job they like. Formal job applications are the first contact with your future employer and they can pave the way to a job interview.

Exercise 2: Read for Information

Look at the cover letter and résumé on pages 66-68. Give the following information about the applicant.

1. name, address, and telephone number of one referee
2. educational background
3. skills, interests, and hobbies
4. reasons why an employer should hire the person
5. name and address of the last employer
6. volunteer or community work
7. type of work done in the past
8. cities in which the person has worked
9. languages spoken
10. training in progress

2473 Maplewood, #205
Toronto, Ontario
M1P 2J7

June 12, 199–

Dear Sir/Madam,

Please accept this application for the position of sales clerk which was advertised in the Toronto Star on Thursday. I feel that I have the qualifications you require. My curriculum vitae gives details of my education and experience. I have a high-school education, and I can speak two languages in addition to fairly good English.

My work experience has not been in department stores, but I have worked as a sales clerk in both Vancouver and Toronto.

I am well organized and punctual. I enjoy meeting the public and I liked my previous jobs. I feel that my enthusiastic manner and friendly personality would make me a good candidate to work in the sportswear department of your store.

I am available for an interview at your convenience. If I am hired, I can begin work immediately.

If you require further information about my past performance, please feel free to contact the people named in my CV. Thank you for your consideration.

Yours sincerely,

Gerry Pinto

Gerry Pinto

CURRICULUM VITAE

Gerry Pinto

Address	2473 Maplewood, #205 Toronto, Ontario M1P 2J7 (416) 392 1546
SIN	221 786 724
Languages	English, Portuguese, some French

EDUCATION

1990	Certificate in Recreation Vancouver Community College
1988	Certificate en français, langue seconde UBC Summer School of French
1988	High School Diploma Oak Bay High School Victoria, BC

JOB EXPERIENCE

April 1992– present	Antonio's Sporting Goods North York Mall, Toronto My duties are serving customers, operating the cash register, stocking the shelves, and making minor repairs to bicycles.
May 1990– January 1992	Vancouver Book Exchange Granville Street, Vancouver I was responsible for serving customers, unpacking books and placing them on the shelves, shipping orders, and labelling merchandise.

-2-

| Sept. 1988– | Burnaby Saddle Shop |
| July 1989 | Wentworth Street, Vancouver |

My job was serving customers, taking orders by phone from stores we sold to, and cleaning up the store and work room.

ACTIVITIES

I was involved with coaching junior tennis in the Vancouver Parks programme, and I am now teaching swimming at the Community Recreation Centre in Scarborough as a volunteer.

I enjoy recreational bicycle riding, camping, and hiking.

I am presently taking a course in book-keeping at Seneca College.

REFERENCES

Ms Jean Wei, Manager
Antonio's Sporting Goods
North York Mall
1764 Bishop Street
Toronto, ON
M2G 1J6
(416) 343 9660

Mr. Tony Green, Coordinator
Community Outreach Project
Community Recreation Centre
Scarborough, ON
M4P 1Y6
(416) 293 3648

Mr. Jack McKenzie, Owner
Burnaby Saddle Shop
1826 Wentworth Street
Vancouver, BC
V4T 6J8
(604) 277 2204

Exercise 3: Use the Information

Work with a partner. Choose one of the ads below. Prepare a résumé and an appropriate cover letter.

SHOE SALES
Shoe salesperson required for children's shoes. Exp. pref. 785-3824

Couriers, cars or bikes. Good earnings. Own vehicle. 921-7689

WAITER/ WAITRESS, steak and seafood restaurant in Oakville. Must be experienced in tableside service. Fax résumé: 487-0916

RECEPTIONIST for dental office. 441- 6779

TRAINEES
Giftware manuf. needs sales trainees. Starting salary $350 wk. no exp. 665-9768

CASHIER for supermarket. Exper. Call Mary: 870-6512

First Impressions

Exercise 1: Get Ready

Discuss these questions in a group.

1. Have you ever been interviewed?
2. What was the interview for?
3. Where did it take place?
4. Who was present?
5. What kind of questions were asked?
6. How would you do things differently in a future interview?

Exercise 2: Discuss

Work in a group. Read the questions about what to do in a job interview. Choose the best answers.

1. When you go to an interview, you should:
   a) go alone
   b) go with a friend
   c) go with a family member

2. If your interview is for 10:00 a.m., you should arrive:
   a) 10 minutes early
   b) exactly at 10:00
   c) at 10:10

3. When you meet the interviewer, you should:
   a) slap the interviewer on the back
   b) shake the interviewer's hand
   c) hug the interviewer warmly

4. If you are a smoker, during the interview you should:
   a) ask if the interviewer minds if you smoke
   b) take out your cigarettes and offer one to the interviewer
   c) refrain from smoking until after the interview

5. During the interview, you should:
   a) put your coat or handbag on the interviewer's desk
   b) lean on the interviewer's desk
   c) sit up straight in your chair

6. If you feel nervous you should try to relax by:
   a) telling jokes to warm up the atmosphere
   b) concentrating on the questions and your answers
   c) mentioning that you really need the job

7. If the interviewer asks why you want the job, you should answer:
   a) "I really need the money at the moment."
   b) "I feel I could do a good job for this company."
   c) "I've heard this company has good benefits."

8. When the interviewer asks questions, you should:
   a) give short answers such as "Yes" and "No"
   b) go into a lot of detail, even if it takes a while
   c) answer the questions as directly as you can

9. Before the interview, you should:

   a) find out about the company and the job you are applying for

   b) prepare some funny stories about your family

   c) prepare a detailed list of duties you are willing to perform

10. If the interviewer looks tired during the interview, you should:

    a) offer to go out to get a coffee

    b) say nothing and continue the interview

    c) ask if the interviewer was up late last night

11. If the interviewer answers a phone call, you should:

    a) offer advice that makes you look intelligent

    b) drum your fingers on the desk and stare at the interviewer

    c) sit quietly and look at something on the wall

12. If the interviewer asks your age, you could say:

    a) "I'd rather not discuss my age."

    b) "It's none of your business."

    c) "I'm 46. How about you?"

13. If you are kept waiting for an interview, you should

    a) go out for a coffee and come back later

    b) clear your throat loudly a few times

    c) read a book or magazine while you wait

14. If the interviewer says, "Thank you very much", you should

    a) get up and leave the office

    b) ask when you start work

    c) smile and wait for instructions

15. When you prepare your CV, you should

    a) exaggerate your accomplishments a little

    b) be completely truthful about everything

    c) leave out details that may be misunderstood

16. You are applying for a job that requires special clothes. At the interview you should:

    a) wear your fanciest clothes to make a good impression

    b) wear the kind of clothes you would wear to work

    c) wear clothes that are neat and clean

Did You Know?   It is illegal for an employer to ask your age or religion in Canada.

The Job Interview

Listening Activity 5

Exercise 1: Get Ready to Listen

Work in a group. Read the questions. Discuss some possible answers. Decide which answers you think would be the best.

1. Why are you interested in working for this company?

2. Have you any experience with this kind of work?

3. Could you tell me a little about how you'd handle someone who was angry or upset with our service?

4. What kind of salary are you expecting?

5. Do you have any questions?

6. Sometimes we need to have our employees work overtime. Would you be available at busy times of the year if it were necessary?

Exercise 2: Listen and Decide

Listen to the interview. As you listen, check (✔) whether each answer is good, acceptable, or bad. Use the worksheet.

	Good	Acceptable	Bad
1. Ms. Lopez Mr. Chang Mr. March			
2. Ms. Murray Ms. Rosen Ms. Lopez			
3. Mr. Chang Mr. Brown Ms. Lopez			
4. Ms. Murray Mr. Chang Mr. Brown			
5. Mr. Brown Mr. Chang Mr. March			
6. Ms. Murray Mr. Brown Ms. Rosen			

Exercise 3: Discuss

□□
□□

Read the answers to the questions. In your group, discuss why you rated the answers as you did.

The Job Interview

1. **Interviewer:** Why are you interested in working for this company, Ms. Lopez?

   Ms. Lopez: Well, I heard they give long vacations and nobody expects you to work too hard. I like that.

   Interviewer: Mr. Chang?

   Mr. Chang: I'm a pretty energetic person. I like to do a good job. You need to work with people at your own level. The last three companies I worked for were no good. They didn't know how to get things done. I don't like working with a bunch of stupid people, you know.

   Interviewer: Mr. March?

   Mr. March: This company has a good reputation. It treats its customers and employees well. I'm a hard worker and I feel I could contribute to this company.

2. **Interviewer:** Have you any experience with this kind of work, Ms. Murray?

   Ms. Murray: Yeah, sure. No problem. I can handle it.

   Interviewer: Ms. Rosen?

   Ms. Rosen: Not exactly the same work, but I have had some related experience. I'm very eager to learn this job.

   Interviewer: Ms. Lopez?

   Ms. Lopez: Ummm, Ahhh… What is this job again?

3. **Interviewer:** Could you tell me a little bit about how you'd handle someone who was angry or upset with our service, Mr. Chang?

   Mr. Chang: I'd ask what the problem was and offer some solutions.

   Interviewer: Mr. Brown?

   Mr. Brown: I'd tell the person what I thought… I'd say: "If you don't like the service, you can go to another store!"

   Interviewer: Ms. Lopez?

   Ms. Lopez: I'd say: "It's not my fault. You'll have to speak to my boss."

4. **Interviewer:** What kind of salary are you expecting, Ms. Murray?

Ms. Murray: Well, I realize I would be a new employee. I wouldn't expect to start with a high salary, but I hope I would do a good job and see my salary increase.

Interviewer: Mr. Chang?

Mr. Chang: Oh. I don't know. Whatever.

Interviewer: Mr. Brown?

Mr. Brown: I have some pretty big expenses coming up. I need to get a good salary. A few grand more than I'm making now, you know. Are there any bonuses I could get right away?

---

5. **Interviewer:** Do you have any questions, Mr. Brown? ... And get your feet off my desk!

Mr. Brown: No.

Interviewer: Mr. Chang?

Mr. Chang: Yes. What kind of vacation plan do you have?

Interviewer: Mr. March?

Mr. March: Yes. How can I learn more about the way the company operates? Do you have any training programmes I'd be eligible for?

---

6. **Interviewer:** Sometimes we need to have our employees work overtime. Would you be available at busy times of the year if this were necessary, Ms. Murray?

Ms. Murray: I realize that there will be exceptional demands occasionally in this kind of work. I assume I would be paid for the overtime.

Interviewer: Mr. Brown?

Mr. Brown: No. My personal time is very important. I'm definitely not into that stuff.

Interviewer: Ms. Rosen?

Ms. Rosen: Yes, certainly. But could you give me an idea of what it entails?

Did You Know? The closest to perfection a person ever comes is when filling out a job application form!

Where Do They Work?

Work with a partner. Match the worker to the workplace.

1.	forest ranger	pharmacy
2.	bell hop	garage
3.	salesperson	barn
4.	druggist	cockpit
5.	chef	showroom
6.	mechanic	kitchen
7.	farmer	limousine
8.	diva	firetower
9.	pilot	prison
10.	maitre d'	opera house
11.	comedian	swimming pool
12.	robot	hotel
13.	chauffeur	night club
14.	warden	hospital
15.	life guard	restaurant
16.	orderly	factory

Who Gets the Job?

 Role Play

Work in groups. Prepare a dialogue to present to the class.

Interviewer: Decide on a job. Prepare questions to ask applicants. You will have three applicants.

Applicants: Prepare answers to the questions that the interviewer will ask.

Class: Listen to the interviews and decide who is the best candidate for the job.

Hire/Higher

Work with a partner. Choose the correct word for each sentence.

1. The job would be easier if they could **hire/higher** more people.
2. The news about the company's losses upset the **hole/whole** staff.
3. Nobody **guest/guessed** that she was the manager of a large hotel.
4. The man said that the cheque was in the **male/mail**.
5. The director is a person with high moral **principals/principles**.
6. Before the meeting begins, someone has to call the **roll/role**.
7. The secretary gave the sales representative a **peace/piece** of her mind.
8. The person with the best sales record **one/won** a prize.
9. The boss said that the coffee **breaks/brakes** were too long.
10. Customers don't like it if they have to **weight/wait**.
11. The manager wanted to **meet/meat** the deadline.
12. We were worried when **our/hour** pay cheques weren't ready.

Senses and Perceptions

The Senses Quiz

Exercise 1: Discuss

What do you know about the senses? Do this quiz and find out.

Discuss these questions in a group. In some cases, more than one answer can be correct. When you have finished, turn to page 91. Read the information to check your answers.

1. Which of these have colour vision?
   a) fish
   b) reptiles
   c) mammals

2. Which part of the body is most sensitive to touch?
   a) the middle of the back
   b) the fingertip
   c) the back of the hand

3. Which part of your tongue will detect the flavour of ice cream first?
   a) the front of the tongue
   b) the sides of the tongue
   c) the back of the tongue

4. Which animals are used to detect illegal drugs because they have a superior sense of smell?
   a) dogs
   b) horses
   c) pigs

5. If you leave a well-lit room and step into the darkness, how long does it take your eyes to adjust to the surroundings?
   a) 15 minutes
   b) 5 minutes
   c) 30 minutes

6. Which of these has the best sense of hearing?
   a) a human
   b) a bat
   c) a dolphin

7. Which of these does your tongue give the least information about?
   a) hot and cold
   b) wet and dry
   c) sweet and sour

8. When is your sense of smell and taste strongest?

   a) at birth

   b) at 20 years of age

   c) at 60 years of age

9. The human eye has one lens. How many lenses does a dragonfly's eye have?

   a) 2

   b) 75

   c) 30 000

10. Which sense is the best developed in the animal kingdom?

    a) smell

    b) touch

    c) hearing

11. Smell is important to humans because:

    a) it warns us of danger

    b) it tells us when food is nearby

    c) it evokes memories and feelings

12. Humans use their noses to smell. What do snakes use?

    a) their tongues

    b) their skin

    c) their mouths

13. Which of these can influence the way a food tastes?

    a) smell

    b) appearance

    c) texture

14. People who are colour-blind have the most trouble distinguishing:

    a) black and white

    b) green and red

    c) blue and green

Did You Know? Humans can recognize over 10 million shades of colour, but these shades are all based on only three primary colours: red, yellow, and blue!

Helen Keller

Listening Activity 6

Exercise 1: Get Ready to Listen

Discuss these questions in a group.

1. What are the five senses?
2. What are some uses of each of the senses?
3. Name some animals that have especially good senses.
4. Which of the senses is the most important for you? Why?
5. Which of the senses is the least important for you? Why?

 ## Exercise 2: Listen for Meaning

Listen to the information. Which of these topics are discussed?

1. how Helen Keller became blind and deaf
2. Anne Sullivan's childhood
3. games Anne Sullivan played with Helen
4. how Helen learned the manual alphabet
5. how Helen learned to swim
6. how Helen learned the meaning of words
7. Helen's travels
8. how Helen learned to listen and speak

⬤⬤ Exercise 3: Listen for Details

Listen to the information. While you listen, answer the questions.

1. Name three ways in which our senses are important to us.
2. How did Helen Keller lose her sight and hearing?
3. How did Helen express herself as a small child?
4. Who helped her find a teacher?
5. How did Anne Sullivan make contact with Helen?
6. Describe the games that Anne Sullivan played with Helen.
7. What is the manual alphabet?
8. Why was Helen able to learn the manual alphabet so quickly?
9. Which words was Anne Sullivan trying to teach Helen in April?
10. Where did Helen and Anne go when Helen became frustrated?
11. What was the first word that Helen understood?
12. What method did Helen use to read and write in the next few years?
13. Why could Helen not use her voice?
14. Why did Helen want to learn to talk?
15. Explain where Helen put each of her fingers in order to hear people talk.
    a) middle finger   b) forefinger   c) thumb
16. What was Helen's first sentence?

Exercise 4: Write

Write about the sense that is most important to you.

A Famous Person

Exercise 1: Prepare a Report

Prepare a report on a famous person of your choice. Plan to speak for about 15 minutes.

Exercise 2: Present

Present an oral report to the class or to your group. Give people a chance to ask you questions.

Exercise 3: Write

Write a summary of the information you gave in your report.

Optical Illusions

Exercise 1: Get Ready

Most of us trust what our eyes tell us. Usually what we think we see and what we do see are not so different. Sometimes, however, we can be fooled by an optical illusion. We may perceive something as being bigger or smaller than it really is or we may see something as nearer or farther. It is also possible to misinterpret what we see. For example, a branch in the forest may look like a snake, or vice versa. We may think we see a big person in the distance, and then realize that what we see is a small person carrying a large object.

Exercise 2: Discuss

Look at the following pictures. With your group, discuss what you see.

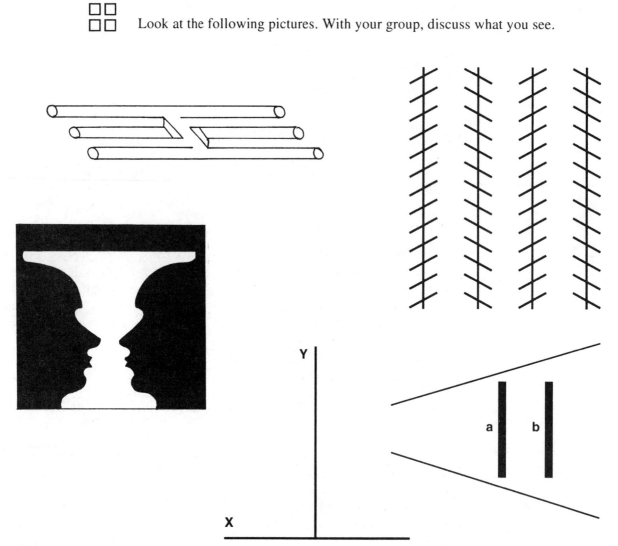

Witness Perception

Exercise 1: Get Ready to Read

Discuss these questions in a group.

1. What do you usually remember about someone you meet for the first time?
2. What kind of visual information do you find easiest to remember?
3. What are some factors that can influence how well we see things?
4. What characteristics do you think make a person a good witness?
5. Have you ever been the witness to a crime?

📖 **Exercise 2: Read Quickly for General Ideas**

Read the text quickly. Find the paragraphs that talk about the following:

1. the impact of emotions on what we remember
2. the reason why we cannot focus on everything at once
3. the way our environment affects our perception
4. the scene of a robbery
5. the way our personal interests influence what we remember
6. the way our physical differences influence how we perceive the world
7. the role of memory in the way we recall things

Witness Perception

A. Imagine this scene. Several people are outside a store that is robbed by a gunman. They witness the robber running out of the store, jumping into a car, and driving off. When the police arrive, the witnesses begin to give their descriptions of what they saw. The gunman was tall, short, and medium height, depending on who you talk to. He had blond hair, dark hair, a beard, or a moustache. He got into a small red car and a large grey car and left with a man and a woman, two men, or alone. The shopkeeper remembers that the gun was big and that the man wore a ring on his little finger.

B. How is this confusion possible? For one thing, there are physical differences in the way any of us perceives the world around. Some people are more sensitive to light, sound, touch, or odour than other people. In addition, there may be external factors that affect how accurately we perceive things. Someone with excellent vision, for instance, may be able to identify colours accurately during daylight. Yet at dusk or at night, the same person's sense of colour-discrimination will be much less accurate. The reason for this is partly that physical changes take place in the eye at night. The part of the eye that can see different colours during the day changes to help the eye adjust to night-time vision. The sense of colour-discrimination is greatly reduced, and what we see is more likely various shades of grey. Night vision can be affected in a second way, too. If we leave a well-lit room and step into the darkness, the eyes make a physical adjustment. It takes about half an hour before the eyes have completely adjusted to the darkness, so we don't see as well as we expect to. Some people also have sight impairments such as colour blindness, which causes certain colours such as green and red to appear as shades of grey.

C. It is well known in police work that eye-witnesses are not always an accurate source of information. Factors such as the time of day or the brightness of sunlight can affect how we see things; so can obstructions such as a tree branch or light post that are in a witness's line of vision. It is also possible for a witness to be misled by an optical illusion. For example, a red object may appear larger than a blue one. The height of an object or person is easy to overestimate and the width is easy to underestimate.

D. Someone who is exposed to many different sights and sounds at the same time can give attention to only a few of them. Let's go back to the witnesses at the robbery. A couple on their way to a restaurant may have been talking about what they were going to eat for dinner, and may have noticed a man with a limp run across the street and drive off with someone in a car. A young man may have been admiring the small red sports car with the motor running that was stopped at the kerb. A woman leaving the store may have noticed something strange about the tall, dark-haired young man at the cash register. Even when we are equally alert, our attention isn't drawn to the same things.

E. Interest determines what we notice, too. One person may be more perceptive about colours, physical appearances, and the presence of people. Another person may be better at describing distances, speeds, and mechanical devices. For example, if a well-dressed woman walked down the street in front of a sidewalk café with a dog on a leash, customers in the café who looked up and saw her would probably be able to describe different things. One person might notice her age and general appearance. This person would, perhaps, be able to give a clearer description of the woman's weight and hair colour than of the dog. Another person looking out from the café might focus on the woman's clothing. This person's description might include details about her suit, shoes, and earrings—items that could have little interest for

someone else. At the same time, a child might be able to give a very good description of the dog, telling its size, colour, and perhaps its disposition, but would probably have very little to say about the woman's suit.

F. Another factor that affects how we perceive things is emotion. One common emotion during a robbery is fear. If you were robbed by an armed man, you would probably remember him as taller and huskier than he really was. It is not uncommon for robbery victims to describe the gun used as very large and black, no matter what size it actually was. It is common, too, for victims to remember one detail such as a missing button on the robber's sleeve, but to be unable to say what colour the clothes were or how tall the robber was.

G. And, finally, memory plays a role in our perceptions. The farther an event is in the past, the more inaccurate our memories become. First, we just don't retain all the details of a situation for more than an hour. Events that are fresh in our minds as they occur begin to fade very quickly. Second, as we rethink the details of an event, we may add details that weren't necessarily there at the time. Other people may make suggestions that become part of our memory. Over time, reality and imagination blend together to alter our portrait of what we saw.

Exercise 3: Read Carefully for Details

Work with a partner. Look in the text for the answers.

1. How did the robber escape?

2. What did the shopkeeper remember?

3. Give two reasons why we don't always perceive the world the same way.

4. Why do we see colours at night differently from the way we see them in the day?

5. How long does it take the eyes to adjust to darkness?

6. Name the sight impairment that is mentioned.

7. What factors can affect the way we see things in the day?

8. Give examples of optical illusions.

9. What did the couple notice at the scene of the robbery?

10. What did the young man notice?

11. Give some examples of how personal interest determines what people notice.

12. If someone in the sidewalk café noticed the woman's general appearance, what might he or she describe?

13. What might a person be able to describe about the woman's clothing?

14. What might the child tell about the dog?

15. Describe a robbery victim's impression of a robber.

16. How long does it take before events begin to fade from our memories?

17. What else happens to our recollection of events over time?

Did You Know?   These pictures show the pupil of a cat's eye. On the left, you can see how the pupil closes to a thin slit when the light is bright. In the centre, you can see how the pupil becomes very large when the light gets dim. Cats also have a reflecting layer inside their eyes that helps them see in dim light.

Exercise 4: Review Ideas

Look in the text to see what is probably true about the robber.

armed / unarmed   young / old / middle-aged

tall / short / medium   big car / small car

fair hair / dark hair   red car / grey car

alone / with someone else

Dolphins

Video Activity 2

Exercise 1: Get Ready to Watch the Video

Work in a group. Make a list of everything you know about dolphins.

Exercise 2: Watch the Video for General Ideas

Watch the video. After you watch, work in a group. Discuss what you have
learned.

Exercise 3: Watch the Video for Details

While you watch the video, answer the questions. Use the worksheet.

1. How many species of dolphins are there?
2. What two suggestions have been made to explain why ancient dolphins moved from the land to the water?
3. Why do dolphins come to the surface?
4. What is the function of a dolphin's blow-hole?
5. How do scientists know whether Tuffy has reached his target?
6. Why do scientists want a specimen of the dolphin's breath?
7. What do the pictures tell scientists about the dolphin's breathing?
8. Describe how dolphins move.
9. How fast can dolphins swim?
10. What name is given to the sound dolphins make?
11. List three things that dolphins learn from echoes.
12. Why does the scientist cover the dolphin's eyes?
13. Which human invention is compared with echolocation?
14. What do dolphins use their eyes to see?
15. What proof do we have that dolphins can recognize shapes?
16. What do dolphins eat?
17. What does a killer whale eat?
18. What is surprising about a killer whale's swimming in shallow water?
19. Name two hunting techniques the killer whale uses to catch the baby sea lion.
20. Why is it difficult to study dolphins?
21. Where do dolphins live?
22. What is a dolphin's life span?
23. What proof is given that dolphin's are social animals?
24. What characteristics do dolphins share with other mammals?
25. What is the first thing a dolphin does when it is born?
26. Who helps the baby get to the surface?
27. List three questions that humans have about dolphins' intelligence.
28. According to the video, why do some dolphins probably seek human company?

Did You Know?   An animal called the bush-baby lives in Africa. A bush-baby's eyes reflect light so strongly at night that you can see them from over 400 metres away.

Exercise 4: Practise Speaking

Tell your partner everything you can remember about the dolphin.

Exercise 5: Write

Write everything you remember about dolphins.

The Senses Quiz: Answers

Exercise 2: Read for Information

Read the information. Check your answers to the questions on pages 79 and 80.

1. People are fortunate in having good colour vision. Fish, birds, and reptiles are usually sensitive to colour, and some insects are able to see colours that people cannot, but colour vision in mammals is rare.

2. In humans, nerve endings convey information through the skin. Different parts of the body are more sensitive to touch than others. For example, the skin on the fingertips, around the lips, and on the bottoms of the feet is crowded with nerve endings. The skin on our backs has only a few nerve endings.

3. There are four different types of taste buds, located on different parts of the tongue. The taste buds at the back of the tongue recognize bitter tastes, such as lemon juice. Sour tastes, such as yoghurt, are detected at the sides of the tongue. Taste buds at the sides of the tongue's front pick up salty tastes. The front of the tongue has the buds that recognize sweet tastes.

4. Most animals have senses of smell and taste that are superior to those of humans. For example, the average dog can smell a million times better than the average human being can. People have often used dogs to hunt for food or criminals, and to help find illegal drugs and explosives. Pigs have also been used. Some people say that pigs do a better job, because they are more intelligent!

5. Physical changes take place in the eye at night. If we leave a well-lit room and step into the darkness, the eyes make a physical adjustment. It takes about half an hour before the eyes have completely adjusted to the darkness, so we don't see as well as we expect to.

6. Dolphins have the best sense of hearing of any animal. Their hearing is twice as good as the hearing of bats, who are second on the list. It is 14 times better than that of humans.

7. The tongue is crowded with sensory receptors, but they are not the kind that feel heat and cold. That is why you can drink a cup of coffee or tea that would burn your fingers. It is easy to scald your tongue with hot liquids because the tongue does not recognize the danger.

8. Your senses of smell and taste fade as you grow older. In fact, they begin to fade as soon as you are born. At the age of 10, you have 82 percent of your original sense of smell and taste left, but by the age of 60, only 38 percent is left. At the age of 80, only 29 percent is left.

9. Most insects, such as the housefly, have eyes that are made up of thousands of tiny lenses. Their eyes are called compound eyes. Strangely enough, the lenses of the housefly cannot focus, so the flies can see clearly only at very close range. Spiders can often have as many as eight eyes set in a ring around their heads. The eyes of the dragonfly have up to 30 000 lenses. The dragonfly relies on its sense of sight alone to catch insects for food.

10. Touch is perhaps the most common sense of all. Even microscopic single-celled creatures respond to physical contact. Insects and crabs are often very sensitive to touch, as physical contact is the first warning they have of the interest of a predator.

11. In humans, smell is the least-developed sense. Yet smell is still important to us. It warns us of danger by detecting smoke or noxious or harmful chemicals in the air. It also signals when food is sour or rotten and should not be eaten. But smell also provokes an emotional response in humans. People often associate odours with memories of the past. For example, baked goods may be associated with happy recollections of home and family.

12. Animals have different ways of sensing smells. Snakes use their tongues; catfish use their whiskers; and insects use their antennae, or feelers. A bird called the kiwi has nostrils that breathe in smells right at the tip of its long beak. And sea anemones trap smells with their waving tentacles.

13. Eating is a complicated activity, and involves the use of many senses together. Smell is very important in giving us information about food. Without smell, we would be unable to tell the difference between a salty cracker and a sweet cookie. A raw potato and an apple would taste the same as well, if we could not smell them. But colour and appearance also alter the way we think a food tastes. For example, in an experiment, blue scrambled eggs were reported to taste worse than normal ones, even though they had merely been coloured with a tasteless food dye. For this reason, the preparation and appearance of food is as important as smell and texture in making food appetizing.

14. Colour-blind people can see clearly, but have trouble distinguishing between certain colours. Red and green usually present the most problems, which means that people who are colour-blind have to be extra careful about reading traffic lights. Fortunately, they can tell the colours by their positions. The red light is always at the top.

Did You Know?   Money is the sixth sense without which we cannot enjoy the other five!

Unit 7

The Environment

Our Fragile Planet

Exercise 1: Discuss

What do you know about problems in our environment? Do this quiz to find out. Work in a group. Choose the best answers.

1. Acid rain is:
   a) a rock group
   b) a new soft drink
   c) rain mixed with pollutants

2. Plastic foam containers and refrigerators both contain:
   a) foods that come from greenhouses
   b) oil that is used for cooking
   c) chemicals that can harm our atmosphere

3. The greenhouse effect is:
   a) a warming of the earth's surface
   b) a place to raise plants
   c) a green building

4. The principal gas that contributes to the greenhouse effect is:
   a) hydrogen
   b) nitrogen
   c) carbon dioxide

5. The ozone layer:
   a) protects the earth from ultraviolet rays
   b) is 10 kilometres above the earth
   c) is below the earth's surface

6. How many lakes have died in Canada as a result of acid rain?
   a) 200
   b) 800
   c) 14 000

7. The letters "CFC" stand for:
   a) the name of a new TV station
   b) a chemical that is destroying our upper atmosphere
   c) a method for cleaning up pollution

8. Which animal is in danger of extinction as a result of pollution?
   a) the moose
   b) the beaver
   c) the beluga whale

9. Which of these is not a fossil fuel?
   a) oil
   b) natural gas
   c) the sun

10. Hazardous waste is:
    a) a song on the radio
    b) garbage we throw away
    c) dangerous chemicals in our environment

11. The amount of garbage the average Canadian household throws away each year is:
    a) 200 kilograms
    b) 800 kilograms
    c) 1200 kilograms

12. Ecology is the study of:
    a) plants and animals
    b) people
    c) both of the above

13. The number of chemicals detected in the Great Lakes is:
    a) 20
    b) 150
    c) 1000

14. Landfills are:
    a) places to dump garbage
    b) places to build a mountain
    c) areas where trees are being planted

15. Cougars and orchids are examples of:
    a) plants and animals from Canada
    b) plants and animals that are endangered
    c) plants and animals that are found everywhere

16. Which of these contribute to deforestation?
    a) camping
    b) logging
    c) manufacturing

Exercise 2: Read for Information

Look at the information that follows. Find the answers to the quiz.

Our Fragile Planet

Royal Bank Reporter

Acid Rain

Acid Rain is caused by emissions of sulphur dioxide and nitrogen oxides from such sources as coal-fired generating stations, ore-smelter smokestacks, and the exhaust pipes of cars, buses, and trucks. The acid gases rise in the atmosphere, and then they are carried vast distances by winds before returning to earth in the form of rain, snow, fog, or dust. The result is serious damage to lakes, trees, crops, wildlife, and buildings. Close to 14 000 lakes in Canada are dead. People, too, may suffer from acid rain, with respiratory ailments or allergic reactions.

Water Pollution

Our oceans, rivers, and lakes are dumping grounds for human sewage and chemicals used by industries. Over 1000 chemicals have been detected in the Great Lakes, which contain 20 percent of the world's fresh water. The Great Lakes are so polluted that fish living in their waters have developed cancerous tumours. In the St. Lawrence River, which feeds into the ocean from the Great Lakes, the beluga whale population is at risk as a result of massive pollution.

Global Warming

This phenomenon is likely because of growing amounts of carbon dioxide in the atmosphere: there has been an increase of 20 percent in the past 200 years. Carbon dioxide emitted from fossil fuels, which accounts for 90 percent of all global energy, is the most significant contributor to the "greenhouse effect": the gas forms a kind of shroud around the earth, thus preventing much of the solar radiation from escaping naturally. The destruction of tropical rain forests also contributes to a climate change, but to a much lesser extent than does the use of oil, coal, and gas as fuel. Global warming would alter our planet drastically, causing massive droughts in some areas, extensive flooding in others, and food shortages worldwide.

Ozone

Ozone is a kind of oxygen formed naturally in the upper atmosphere. The natural ozone layer filters out harmful amounts of ultraviolet light generated by the sun. Certain chemicals—most notably chlorofluorocarbons (CFCs)—attack the protective ozone layer, thus allowing more ultraviolet light to reach the earth. The depletion of the ozone layer increases the risks of skin cancer and eye cataracts in humans; it also results in damage to crops and aquatic life. Major sources of CFCs are refrigeration systems and the manufacture of plastic foam products. Once in the atmosphere, CFCs can eat away at the ozone layer for 100 years.

What's What: A Glossary of Ten Commonly Used Environmental Terms

Biodegradable: Something capable of being broken down by bacterial processes into basic elements or compounds. "Biodegradable" plastics, however, are merely reduced to a plastic dust, at best.

Biosphere: The regions of earth where life can exist, including the soil, water, and lower atmosphere.

Ecology: The scientific study of living things (humans, animals, and plants) in relation to one another and their environment.

Endangered species: Animals and plants that are in danger of becoming extinct; the *Status of Endangered Wildlife in Canada* currently lists 20 animal and 17 plant species threatened with imminent extinction in the Canadian wild.

Fossil fuels: Fuels such as coal, oil, or natural gas that have been formed from fossil remains of ancient plant and animal life.

Hazardous wastes: Materials that are dangerous to humans, wildlife, and the environment at large and require special disposal techniques. Examples include PCBs, waste pesticides, used oils, and spent solvents.

Landfills: Garbage dumps that are usually pits into which waste is tipped and covered with soil.

Nonrenewable energy sources: Sources that cannot renew themselves or be replaced once they are used. Examples include coal and oil.

Organically grown food: Food grown without use of chemical fertilizers, pesticides, or herbicides.

Renewable energy sources: Sources that can renew themselves or be replaced. Examples include solar energy and wood.

Hazardous Wastes

Over 70 000 chemicals are in use today, with another 1000 being added every year. Chemical spills into waterways destroy fish and plants. Pesticides used in farming run into groundwater and turn up in drinking wells. Chemicals are everywhere, from the fruit we eat, to the solvent used to dry-clean our clothes, to the materials in our carpets and furniture. Most of the chemicals with which we come into contact have never been tested to see if they cause cancer or other problems in humans.

Deforestation

The world's forests are being depleted at an alarming rate. Eleven to 15 million hectares of forests are lost to logging each year—equivalent to an area the size of India in 30 years. More than one-third of the rain forests in the world have already gone. Woodland slopes as far apart as Nepal and Haiti are bare. Deforestation contributes not only to global warming, but also to soil erosion.

Endangered Plants and Animals

From the eastern cougar in Canada to orchids in Brazilian rain forests, countless species of plants and animals are endangered. As their habitats are decimated by voracious loggers and landless peasants, and further eroded by urban sprawl and industrialization, thousands of species vanish each year. In the next 20 years, over one-fifth of all species of plants and animals may disappear.

Garbage

North Americans throw away 800 kilograms of garbage each year, which includes more than 120 kilograms of paper and 450 kilograms of steel—about four times the amount used by citizens in other parts of the world. New York City is building a mountain of trash on Staten Island. In ten years, it will be a monument to our throw-away society—the highest point between Maine and Florida.

"It's the only planet we have got, after all."

William Golding, British novelist and Nobel Prize winner

Waste Not, Want Not

Read the paragraphs from the *Royal Bank Reporter* below. Choose the best word to complete each space.

There is a well-known proverb that says, "Waste not, want not." Today, it is a

proverb that can very well be applied to the environment. The environment is

the very air we **1**_____ , the water we drink, the food we eat,
(see, breathe, exhale, have)

the **2**_____ we walk on. Because the environment knows no
(sidewalk, road, ground, feet)

national **3**_____ , global problems such as climate change,
(flags, days, boundaries, pride)

ozone depletion, and acid rain are **4**_____ issues for people
(pressing, minor, small, new)

everywhere.

Although there is a growing awareness of the important role that

governments, industries, and individuals can play in protecting the

5_____ , the idea of conserving resources and
(economy, trees, rivers, environment)

minimizing **6**_____ is not yet an integral part of everyone's way of
(waste, water, air, smog)

thinking. If you ask most North Americans **7**_____ they are
(that, when, whether, which)

environmentalists, the chances are that they will **8**_____ that they are.
(tell, ask, deny, say)

If you ask them to be specific about steps they are taking to conserve and

9_____ the environment, they may be a little unsure.
(protect, damage, clean, photograph)

People's ways of thinking **10**_____ changing. At the same time,
(will, are, can, is)

however, North Americans, who make up 8 percent of the world's population,

are responsible for 50 percent of its **11**_____ . They are
(food, garbage, time, age)

responsible for 30 percent of the world's energy consumption, as well. It has

been estimated that, with a population of only 26 million people, Canada

12_____ as much impact on the environment as India, which has a
(has, is, was, had)

population of 800 million people. Faced with **13**_____ statistics, it
(some, any, these, them)

might be particularly important for North Americans who want to protect their

children's future to remember that well-known proverb.

Good Planets Are Hard to Find

Listening Activity 7

Interview with Joanne Mills, Environmental Columnist

Exercise 1: Get Ready to Listen

Discuss these questions in a group.

1. Do you think that people today are more concerned about the environment than they were in the past?

2. Can you think of any individuals or organizations that are involved in protecting the environment?

3. What are some things that you do, or that people you know do, to help the environment?

4. Where can you get information about helping the environment?

Did You Know? There is a popular environmental slogan: "Think globally, act locally." This slogan means that we should understand that environmental problems affect the world as a whole, but that we can each work in our own way to help solve them.

[○ ○] **Exercise 2: Listen for Meaning**

Listen to the interview. Which of these topics are discussed?

1. things people can do to help the environment
2. causes of global warming
3. evidence of people's concern about the environment
4. what politicians will do in the next decade
5. how one family helps the environment
6. environmental disasters around the world

[○ ○] **Exercise 3: Listen for Details**

Listen to the interview. While you listen, answer the questions.

1. When did Joanne Mills first become interested in nature?
2. What are some changes she began to notice over the years?
3. What did she hear about that made her feel sad?
4. What caused her to become interested in finding solutions?
5. What did she find particularly interesting about what the naturalist said?
6. What does Joanne Mills think is the most important concern people should have?
7. What does she recommend to avoid being discouraged about the future?
8. Give some examples of things you can do to help the environment.
9. How does she recommend you get started when there is so much to do?
10. What example does she give to show how people today are more interested in the environment?
11. What are some of the actions her family takes to conserve water?
12. What does the Mills family do with food waste?
13. How does Joanne Mills try to reduce the amount of waste?
14. Where can you get more information about the environment?
15. Give examples of things you can do that are just common sense.

Did You Know? The *Canadian Green Consumer Guide* is a book that recommends products and gives information about activities that can help to solve environmental problems.

How Green Are You?

Exercise 1: Discuss

Have you changed any of your habits for more environmentally friendly ones? To help you answer that question, try this quick quiz, which was prepared by Joanne Mills.

For each question answer "A" for **Yes** or **Always**, "B" for **Maybe** or **Occasionally**, or "C" for **No** or **Never**. If a question doesn't apply to you, give yourself the benefit of the doubt and answer it with an "A" or "B." When you have finished, turn to page 103 to check your score.

Energy

1. Have you significantly cut the amount of time you drive your car by using your legs, a bike, a car pool, or public transport instead?
2. Do you regularly tune-up your car to reduce fuel consumption?
3. Is your home adequately and properly insulated?
4. Do you practise a "no person—no power" rule in your home, according to which all lights, radios, TVs, etc. must be turned off when the last person leaves the room?
5. Have you started to buy the new energy-efficient light bulbs (such as the new compact fluorescents) to replace burnt-out ones in your home?
6. Do you make energy-efficiency a top consideration in the purchase of all appliances, whether it's a kettle, washing machine, or car?

Shopping

7. When grocery shopping, do you routinely avoid over-packaged items to reduce the amount of garbage you produce?
8. Have you expressed your concern to your grocery-store manager about the use of polystyrene packaging in the fruit, vegetable, and meat sections?
9. Do you supply your own bags when shopping?
10. Have you lowered your meat consumption and switched to other protein sources that require less energy, land, and water to produce?

11. Do you buy recycled paper products (e.g., toilet paper, insulation, or writing paper)?

Water Conservation

12. Do you fix all leaking taps and toilets as soon as you are aware of them?
13. Do you turn off the tap to conserve water when brushing your teeth, shaving, or washing your hands?
14. Have you installed water conservation devices in your toilet tanks or on your sink, shower, and tub faucets?
15. Do you minimize the amount of water used when watering your lawn or washing your car?

Kitchen

16. Do you use reusable items, such as dishes with lids or plastic milk bags, for lunch or leftovers instead of plastic wrap, aluminum foil, or store-bought bags?
17. Do you use cloth napkins instead of paper ones?
18. Do you use cloth rags to wipe up spills instead of paper towels?
19. Have you eliminated toxic home cleansers and replaced them with more benign, environmentally safe alternatives?
20. Do you use a compost heap to reduce your household garbage?

General

21. Are you an active participant of a recycling programme?
22. When something breaks, do you try to get it repaired instead of throwing it out?

23. Do you recycle old clothes by passing them on to a charity or selling them in a second-hand store or garage sale?

24. Do you use natural garden- and lawn-care techniques instead of toxic chemical fertilizers and pesticides?

25. In the past year, have you planted a tree or contributed to a tree planting?

26. Are the anti-pollution devices on your car properly installed and in working order?

27. Do you write letters to companies and government officials outlining your concerns and asking them to make their products, services, or departments more environmentally friendly?

28. Have you attended or taken part in an environmental activity, campaign, eco-fair, Earth Day event, etc. this year?

29. Do you financially support an environment or conservation group working to save the planet?

30. Do you save hazardous chemicals, such as paint-thinner and car oil, for a toxic waste pick-up day or take them to a special depot, instead of dumping them down the drain or throwing them in the garbage?

Did You Know? Joanne Mills and other environmentalists recommend writing letters as an effective way to help solve environmental problems. You can write to companies to complain about products that are overpackaged or that harm the environment. You can also write to government agencies, asking about their policies on specific issues such as ozone depletion. Ask for a reply. Government agencies consider that every letter they receive represents the viewpoint of many people.

Exercise 2: Use the Information

Make three resolutions about helping the environment in each of the categories below. Discuss how you will implement each one.

Individually	In class

Problems and Solutions

Write about some of the problems in our environment, and some solutions.

How Green Are You?: Scores

Give yourself five points for every "A" answer, two points for every "B," and zero for each "C."

If you scored from 120 to 150: Congratulations! Thanks to people like you, the future is looking brighter.

If you scored from 60 to 119: Good work, but it's going to take more to turn things around.

If you scored from zero to 59: Your effort is simply not enough, for this is not a battle only a few can fight. We need you. Please get involved.

Do this survey again at the end of the year to see if you've been able to increase your score.

Unit 8

Our Daily Lives

Indispensable Inventions

Exercise 1: Get Ready

□□
□□ Discuss these questions in a group.

1. Name some machines and inventions that you use every day.

2. Name some inventions from the twentieth century that have changed our lives.

3. Which machines or inventions do you find most useful?

4. Are there any machines or inventions that you find difficult to use, or that you don't like to use?

Exercise 2: Read and Discuss

□□ Through the ages, human ingenuity has led to the invention of many marvellous things. Read these clues about different inventions. Then work with a partner to answer the questions at the end of each paragraph.

1. In 1928, an American named Richard Drew had the idea of coating thin strips of plastic film with rubber glue. His idea stuck, and his invention is now indispensable in offices, homes, and schools everywhere. Paper wouldn't stay together as well without it. What did he invent?

2. In the winter of 1925, people were amazed to see a strange-looking truck moving slowly down the road. In the front it had two rotating blades, attached to an ejection pipe that spewed out snow. The path behind the truck was clean and smooth. What is this great Canadian invention?

3. Listen through the ear-piece. Talk through the mouth-piece. Simple instructions, perhaps, but very necessary. In its earliest versions, the same part of the machine was used for both talking and listening. During an animated conversation, a person might find herself using her ear to talk and her mouth to listen. This led to conversations that did not make much sense at all. What invention was being used?

4. In 1882, a very practical electrical appliance was invented. It would heat up if plugged in, and was used to take the wrinkles out of clothes. No one bought it, however, because it had one major problem. What is the machine? What was the problem?

5. This method of moving from one floor of a building to another was invented in Britain. Because people were afraid to step onto it, no one would use it. A man named Bumper Harris was hired to demonstrate its use and convince people of its safety. When he got to the top, he waved to the people below. What was the invention?

6. An invention by Charles Fenerty of Nova Scotia formed the basis of one of Canada's largest industries. Mr. Fenerty got his idea during a walk in the woods, around 1830. He noticed that wasps were chewing wood fibres and using the produce to construct their nests. Until this time, rags had been used to manufacture this product. What did Charles Fenerty invent?

7. Using this invention, people could preserve meat, fruits, and vegetables for a long time. There was one problem with this invention, however: getting the food out. The instructions on this invention said: Cut around the top with a hammer and chisel. What was the product? What other product was needed to use it efficiently?

Hello!

Read this paragraph quickly. Then find words or expressions to match the words listed below.

Alexander Graham Bell may have invented the telephone, but he never invented a word to use with it. When speaking into the telephone, he often used the word "Ahoy." The word "Hello" was invented by Bell's rival, Thomas Alva Edison. Edison envisioned that the telephone would be used primarily as a business device. He thought that the lines would remain open permanently. If this were the case, how would anyone know when another party wanted to speak? He chose "Hello" as a way for the caller to announce that he or she wanted to speak.

1. talking
2. competitor
3. predicted
4. mainly
5. tool
6. person

Did You Know? The bathtub came into use in 1850. The telephone was invented in 1874. This means that for almost 25 years, you could have sat in the bathtub without being interrupted by a ringing telephone!

The Sound of the Beep

Listening Activity 8

Exercise 1: Get Ready to Listen

Discuss these questions in a group.

1. Do you have a telephone answering machine? If you do, why did you buy it?

2. If you do not have a telephone answering machine, do you plan to get one in the future? Why or why not?

3. How do you react when you call someone and hear a recording from a machine?

4. Have you heard any unusual messages on telephone answering machines? Describe them.

5. What is your opinion of voice mail or automated telephone messages?

Exercise 2: Listen for Meaning

Listen to the information. What is the main idea?

a) how people feel about telephone answering machines

b) how voice mail will be used in the future

c) how to put a message on a telephone answering machine

Exercise 3: Listen for Details

Listen to the information. While you listen, answer the questions.

1. How do people instinctively react to a ringing telephone?
2. What did Alexander Graham Bell do in his lab after he had invented the telephone? Why?
3. List some negative aspects of the telephone.
4. How long has the telephone answering machine been in existence?
5. Why do some people hate telephone answering machines?
6. Describe two ways in which these people react to the machines.
7. Why do some people suffer from stage fright when confronted with a telephone answering machine?
8. How do people sometimes act when programming an answering machine?
9. Give examples of the types of messages people put on their machines.
10. Why are people who leave messages in positions of power?
11. What dilemma do people face when they bring a guest home and there are messages on their machine?
12. According to etiquette books, what is acceptable with regard to telephone answering machines?
13. What do the etiquette books say about telling jokes on the machine?
14. What progeny of answering machines do we now have to deal with?
15. Explain what we need to do to use this system.
16. Name some situations where these systems are used.
17. What characteristics of answering machines could make them seem almost human in the future?

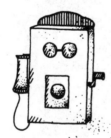

Did You Know? The average person in North American spends two years of his or her life returning telephone calls. Unfortunately, there is only a 27 percent chance of reaching a businessperson on the first phone call!

Cleaning Up

Exercise 1: Discuss

Look at these pictures of machines used in homes in the past. Although they look ancient to us, in 1907 they were the latest in high technology!

Work in a group. Discuss what you think each machine was used for.

Exercise 2: Read

☐☐ Choose the correct words to complete the passage.

Cleaning Up

The world is a dusty, dirty place, and cleaning __1_____ the mess has
    (under, over, up, if)
always been drudgery. Long __2_____ , people beat their rugs
    (ago, after, time, years)
outdoors to rid them of dust. __3_____ , in the mid-nineteenth century,
    (Next, Then, So, Also)
two versions of the carpet-cleaner were invented. __4_____
    (One, Another, Other, Others)
consisted of brushes that whisked the dirt up. The __5_____ used a
    (one, another, next, other)
bellows-like contraption to suck the dirt up.

The invention __6_____ electric motors ushered in a new era of carpet
    (by, at, in, of)
cleaning. One contraption blew air onto the carpet and tried to bounce the dirt into
a box. __7_____ , most of the dust escaped, and
    (Happily, Unfortunately, Luckily, Lastly)
covered the user with grime. Then an Englishman named Cecil Booth had a better
idea. __8_____ placing a handkerchief over his mouth, he lay
    (After, Since, With, Until)
__9_____ on the carpet and began to inhale. Just as he had
    (over, just, others, down)
envisioned, the dirt was sucked up and caught __10_____ the handkerchief. By
    (to, go, in, fast)
1901, Booth had built the first vacuum cleaner, modelled __11_____ the
    (after, through, by, off)
handkerchief version.

Booth's first vacuum cleaner was __12_____ exactly convenient to
    (no, not, ever, always)
use. Large and cumbersome, it had to be towed from house to house by a team of
horses. The horses waited patiently outside __13_____
    (while, since, because, sometimes)
enormous hoses snaked into the houses and sucked up the dirt. The roaring motor
was so loud that people complained that their own horses were frightened. A few
years __14_____ , a quieter miniature version of the vacuum cleaner
    (then, later, before, over)
was invented, and the rest is history.

Exercise 3: Use Vocabulary

Work in a group. Find these parts of some common household appliances.

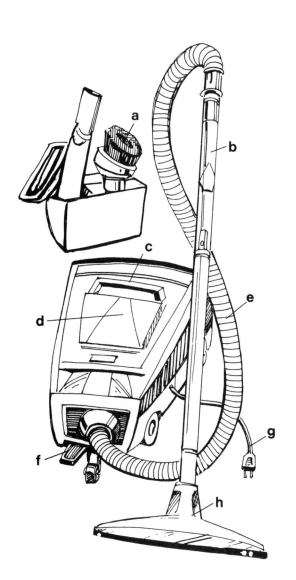

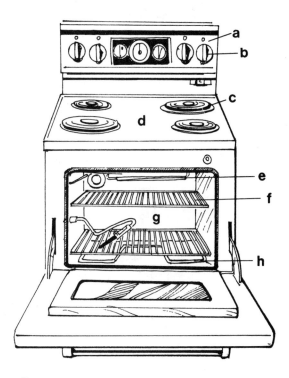

Stove

element	bake element
cooktop	broil element
rack	control knob
oven	control panel

Microwave oven

hinge	handle
control panel	window
clock timer	

Vacuum cleaner

rug and floor nozzle
handle
hood
retractable cord
pipe
flexible hose
switch
dusting brush

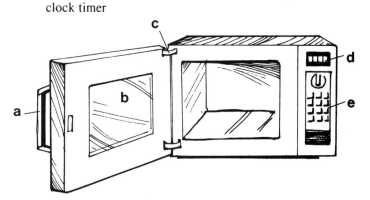

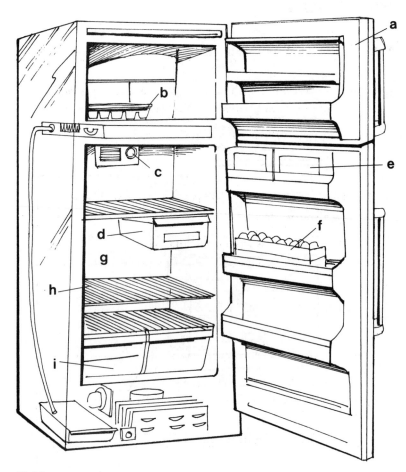

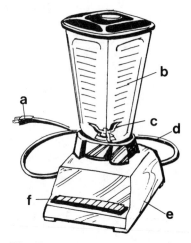

Blender
motor unit
cutting blade
container
pulse buttons
cord
plug

Dishwasher
cutlery basket
rack
worktop surface
detergent dispenser
hinge

Fridge

ice-cube tray
freezer door
butter compartment
egg tray
refrigerator compartment

thermostat control
crisper
shelf
meat keeper

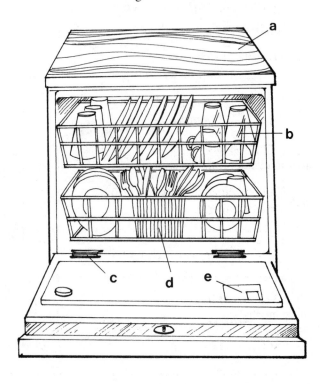

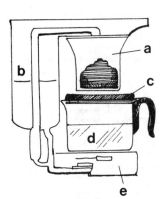

Coffee maker
reservoir
lid
warming plate
basket
carafe

In Times Gone By

Exercise 1: Get Ready to Read

Work in a group. Discuss how you think each task below was accomplished at different times, and how it might be accomplished in the future.

Make a chart to organize your ideas. Be as creative as you can.

	In the 1890s	In the 1990s	In the 2090s
Washing clothes		washing machine	
Drying clothes	hung outside		
Washing dishes			
Getting food			
Preparing and cooking food			
Storing food			
Getting toys and other gifts			
Heating homes			
Travelling in a city or town			
Long-distance travel			
Communicating between homes or workplaces			
Getting information about the world			
Working (kinds of jobs)			
Recreation			

In Times Gone By

Joanne Mills

The Gazette, Montreal

How did people survive in the old days before mega-malls, electricity and throwaways? Ask someone like 91-year-old Evelyn Rose. For those of her generation and the ones that came before, conservation was a basic necessity.

Growing up on a dairy farm outside Corinth, Vt., at the turn of the century, Rose learned the art of reusing items because manufactured products and materials were too scarce to squander. Once she inherited a treasured black silk skirt from an aunt who died. "Nothing was thrown away, things were made over," she said. When the skirt was altered for a better fit, she decided to update the style a bit and add some buttons. The only problem was that the store with the buttons was over 20 miles away by horse and buggy. So she improvised by taking dried beans from the kitchen larder and covering them with black silk. They worked beautifully and cost nothing.

Altering clothes was a standard practice. New collars and shirt cuffs replaced frayed ones, and belts, buttons and bows were used to spruce up old dresses. Even men's old coats were reworked into warm winter outfits for children. Any leftover pieces of material were invariably woven into rag rugs or sewn into patchwork quilts.

But there came a time when even those items wore out and were tossed on the rag pile. That's where Joe came in. Joe was a travelling pedlar who, according to Rose, "showed up at our door every spring just as the buds had opened on the trees," with his cart full of brooms and kitchen utensils. His visits were always special and the family would invite him to spend the night and share his news. In exchange for their hospitality, he would present them with a new tin canister or a pan for the kitchen.

But Joe did more than sell new things. During Joe's visit, Rose's mother would bring out all of her old used rags and rubber boots, which the pedlar bought for a few pennies a pound. The worn material was turned into rag paper and the rubber (a very valuable commodity) was likewise recycled into other products.

Electricity, so abundant today, was nonexistent on the farm but they made do without it. The family relied on coal-oil lamps for their light, but with the store so far away, they would sometimes run out of fuel before the appointed trip to town. In such cases they relied on "sputters." Simply made, sputters consisted of a wick threaded through an ordinary button so that there was a piece standing up a bit. The button was then placed on some fat or oil, whichever was handier, and the wick was set alight. "It would burn," Rose explains, "but it would sputter."

Laundry was hand-washed in a special pot on the stove. The only family Rose knew who had a "washing machine" were the people down the road, and their unit consisted of a large wash tub with two paddles inside. To work it, two of the boys stood on opposite sides and tugged at separate handles to make the paddles inside agitate and wash the clothes. Machine or no, everyone relied on the sun to dry their clothes——summer and winter. On cold winter wash days, "you could bring the long underwear inside and stand it up anywhere," she muses.

The children were also good at making their own toys. In winter, they'd make sleds called "scooters" by using part of a barrel as the runner and bracing a seat in the middle. Sticks became dolls, empty wooden thread spools turned into spinning tops, and willow branches made great whistles.

Back in those days, people weren't so quick to discard good food, either. Most families grew their own food but they also relied on the items nature provided. Dandelions weren't considered a weed, but an important part of the diet, especially after the long winter months when there were few, if any, fresh green vegetables. As soon as the dandelion leaves had grown large enough, they would be picked, washed, boiled and served along with the meat and potatoes for dinner.

Good habits die hard and Rose hasn't left her conservation habits behind. Granddaughter Terry Geller tells how her grandmother still reuses bags and turns old pieces of clothing and material into new items for her great-grandchildren. "What are you saving that for Grandma?" is a frequently repeated question. "Whatever it is," boasts the proud great-grandmother, "I can find another use for it."

Exercise 3: Read Carefully for Details

Work with a partner. Look in the text for the answers.

1. Where and when did Evelyn Rose grow up?
2. Why did Evelyn Rose reuse many things?
3. Describe how each of these items was reused.
    a) a skirt that was outdated
    b) partly worn-out shirts
    c) old dresses
    d) men's old coats
    e) leftover or worn material
4. Who was Joe? Why did his visits cause excitement?
5. What happened to used rags and old rubber boots?
6. How did the family light their home?
7. What did they use if they ran out of fuel?
8. How did Evelyn Rose's family wash clothes?
9. Describe the washing machine that was used by Rose's neighbours.
10. What was the problem with drying clothes in the winter?
11. Describe how each of these toys was made:
    a) sleds
    b) dolls
    c) tops
    d) whistles
12. When were dandelions an important food?
13. How were dandelions prepared?
14. How does Evelyn Rose continue to practise her conservation habits today?

Exercise 4: Write

Write either about a day in the life of your grandparents when they were young or a day in the life of someone 40 or 50 years in the future.

IRON   LARD LAMP   BUTTER CHURN   ICE CREAM MAKER

How Do You Do It?

Exercise 1: Prepare a Report

Prepare a report on how to do something. Choose one of the following topics.

1. how to operate a piece of equipment
2. how to play a game or sport
3. how to cook a particular dish
4. how to fix something
5. how to build something

Exercise 2: Present

Present an oral report to the class or to your group. Give people a chance to ask you questions.

Exercise 3: Write

Write a summary of the information you gave in your report.

Unit 9

Going Places

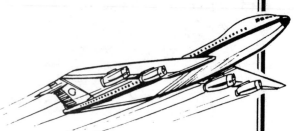

Air Travellers Have Lost It All

Exercise 1: Get Ready to Read

Canada is a vast country that stretches across a continent. Taking the train from Halifax to Vancouver used to be the only way to go from one coast to another. The trip took five full days. Transcontinental travel by car is relatively new in Canada. Before the 1960s, there was no highway through the Rocky Mountains, so people had to take the train. Today, people who travel for business or to visit friends and relatives often prefer to fly.

Exercise 2: Read for Information

Work with a partner. Look in the text for the answers to these questions.

1. List some items people have lost on airlines.
2. Describe the "famous stuffed armadillo story."
3. Why is it often difficult to return lost items?
4. How does Alice Dupere proceed when she tries to identify the owners of lost items?
5. Why is it usually hard to match a lost coat to an owner?
6. What happens to items that are not returned to their owners?
7. List some steps people can take to improve the odds of recovering lost items.
8. Why should you not put the address of your destination on your clothing or other items?
9. Why should you report a loss to the airline as soon as possible?
10. If you lose something in a Canadian airport, where should you go to look for it?
11. Why do some people not want to have goods returned?
12. What was wrong with the insurance claim for the lost camera?

Air Travellers Have Lost It All

David Gersovitz
Canadian Press

Airline travellers lose the wildest things ——from peg legs to silver-plated tubas. They lose eyeglasses by the hundreds, and occasionally a glass eye. It may be hard to forget a 34-kilogram drill bit, but one Air Canada passenger did.

In one year Air Canada picks up enough clothing to stock a department store and enough golf clubs, hockey sticks and skis to open a sporting-goods outlet. Umbrellas? Dozens.

Every so often, someone leaves a wheelchair. Or a baby's crib——although, thank God, never a baby.

The all-time favourite for Tom Illing was the armadillo. "We call it our famous stuffed armadillo story," chuckled Illing, a senior manager whose duties include overseeing the airline's lost-and-found operations.

Several years ago, a large box was sent to Air Canada's main lost-and-found storage room in Montreal. The box was full of paper and the room wasn't well lit. "The person unpacking the box got near the bottom, suddenly saw two beady eyes staring up and let out a scream," Illing recalled.

Everyone came running. They saw the same beady eyes. It was a while before someone edged close enough to discover a real——but quite stuffed ——armadillo.

Air Canada recovers about 11,000 items a year that passengers forget. Not only do passengers lose a lot of things, some make it difficult for the airlines to return them.

Imagine racks full of expensive coats and a two-metre-high double cabinet full of cameras, and you can see what Alice Dupere has to cope with in the Montreal lost-and-found centre. None of the items have identification.

Dupere tries to match a passenger's report of a loss with a found item, or trace the owner where there is evidence to go on.

Many people can't even remember their coat size and become agitated when Dupere questions them about things like the contents of pockets. "They say, 'Look, I lost a Croydon coat——I know it's a Croydon and it's beige.'

"Well," said Dupere, pointing to a long rack of coats, "I have quite a collection of beige coats——and 90 per cent of them are Aquascutum or Croydon."

After a few days in the city where they were found, lost items are forwarded to Montreal, where they generally stay for three to four months. After that, they're auctioned off or given to charity.

There's a simple way for air travellers to improve the odds of recovering lost valuables: Put some ID on them. Tuck a business card in an inside pocket of an overcoat. Tag a camera bag, or better yet, write or tape your name, address and phone number on the inside.

Always put your permanent address on the identification, rather than your immediate destination. Travellers frequently change itineraries. In case of a loss, tell your family or office where the airline can reach you.

And report a loss as soon as possible. If you're still at the airport, it's no problem for the airline to send an employee back on board to retrieve the article. Airports also have lost-and-found departments. If you forget something in a restaurant or at the security checkpoint in a Canadian airport, it will be sent to the airport's lost-and-found, not your airline's.

The smallest clue helps in returning an item. Air Canada was able to track down the owner of a fur-collared coat because there was a card in the pocket from a Los Angeles restaurant. The maitre d' knew right away from the description whom the coat belonged to, Illing said.

Of course, not everyone wants goods returned. Some play a game called Gouge the Insurance Company. Last year, Dupere received a letter from an insurance company reporting that a policy-holder had filed a claim for a camera lost on a particular Air Canada flight. The description matched a camera in Dupere's cabinet. But the passenger, when first reporting the loss, had only left the airline a name—no address or phone number. Dupere got a phone number from the insurance company and informed the man of his good fortune. He vehemently denied the camera was his. "But it is yours," Dupere told him. "It can't be," he replied. "I saw someone steal it during the flight." Why didn't he tell the flight attendants? "I was busy washing my face," he said.

Dupere wrote the insurance company to say the camera had been returned. "You know what? The guy had claimed $1,800, and you should have seen what an old camera it was!"

When You Travel by Air

Discuss these questions in a group.

1. Have you ever travelled by airplane?
2. Have you ever left anything on an airplane?
3. How did you get it back?
4. How can you pass the time on a long flight?
5. Do you find it easy to sleep on a plane?
6. Have you ever experienced jet lag?
7. How can you get over jet lag?

Did You Know?   Canada had many pioneers in aviation. Unfortunately, these early flyers did not have an easy beginning. The public often ridiculed them. If they met a flyer, people would flap their arms like wings, or roll their eyes skyward. They called the first flyers "crazy birdmen." Little did they realize how many of us would soon travel by air!

Travelling Light

Exercise 1: Get Ready to Read

☐☐ Work with a partner. Decide whether these statements are true (**T**) or false (**F**).

1. Jet lag affects everyone who travels long distances by air.

2. Exercise and diet can help you recover from jet lag.

3. The fastest way to recover from jet lag is to get a good night's sleep when you arrive at your destination.

4. Sleep can be affected by using caffeine or alcohol.

5. Sleeping pills can help with jet lag.

6. Listening to cassette tapes with a walkman will keep you awake.

7. Earplugs are sometimes useful in helping you fall asleep.

8. Pills can be used to regulate your internal body clock.

Exercise 2: Read Quickly to Check Predictions

Read quickly to check your true/false predictions.

Travelling Light

Kathleen Doheny
Los Angeles Times

First-class passengers on Air New Zealand are offered more than blankets and pillows to ease the effects of long-distance trips without much sleep. They get a "Revival on arrival" flight kit. Inside are two bottles, one labelled "Awake" and the other "Asleep", containing a blend of fragrances made from plant-based oils.

When trying to stay awake after they land, they use the appropriate aromatherapy in a bath or shower (or dab it on a handkerchief and inhale), according to an airline spokesman. They use the opposite formula when trying to fall asleep.

Some sleep experts aren't convinced that aromatherapy works. But airline officials say the public response has been positive, with passengers grateful for the effort to remedy an age-old problem: the disruption of sleep during and after long-distance travel and the difficulty many people have in sleeping away from home.

"Jet lag affects about three out of four (long-distance) travellers," said Michael Stevenson, a psychologist and clinical director of the North Valley Sleep Disorders Centre in Mission Hills, Calif. But jet lag is just one of the sleep-related problems associated with the difficulties of getting a good night's sleep on the road.

As scientists learn more about the workings of our internal clocks, they can recommend measures to help us arrive at our destinations feeling refreshed. To help us cope with travel-related sleep problems, including jet lag and its prevention, some experts now recommend resetting our clocks by using light therapy, diet, exercise, short-term medication or a combination of those approaches.

"When your body wants to sleep and you want to stay awake, go out into the sun," Stevenson tells travellers. "That will help you move to the other time zone." This light therapy will reset your clock to the destination time, he explained, because light normally helps your brain know what time it is.

When you arrive at your destination, stay up if it is not bedtime there,

Stevenson said. Go to a sidewalk cafe for breakfast. Soak up sunlight. "If you fly from west to east, you want to wake up earlier, so be sure you get lots of sun early in the morning," Stevenson said. If you fly from east to west, he advised getting sun late in the afternoon to help reset the internal clock.

Such use of light therapy, Stevenson said, stems from studies in which researchers discovered that infantrymen, outside much of the day, adjusted more rapidly than commanding officers, who were involved in war-time strategy sessions inside the bunkers. More recent studies have also proved the value of natural-light therapy.

Avoiding excessive caffeine or alcohol, as well as long naps, can minimize travel-related sleep problems, too, Stevenson said. Once you arrive, seek out others.

"Interaction with other people who are on the other (destination) time zone can help," he said. Picking up on their energy, or lack of it if they are winding down for sleep, can be infectious, he said.

Sleeping pills can help some travellers get a good night's sleep, said Dr. Stuart Yudofsky, professor and chairman of psychiatry at Baylor College of Medicine, Houston, and co-author of *What You Need To Know About Psychiatric Drugs* (Ballantine).

Judicious use is the key, agreed Yudofsky and Stevenson. "Some travellers do well on Halcion (triazolam)," Yudofsky said. "Others have severe problems with amnesia." The use of Halcion is highly controversial. Some experts claim it can cause violent behavior; others claim it is safe when prescribed and taken properly.

Before Yudofsky prescribes a sleeping pill for use during travel, he prefers that his patients take the pill on a trial basis during a period in which the patients are not travelling. Then he closely monitors the person, assessing performance the next day and, in particular, watching for memory lapses.

"I do not make the trip the experiment," he said. Some travellers use sleeping pills two or three times a year during long-distance trips very successfully, he said.

Once at your destination, common sense measures can also help minimize sleep disruption. Good sleep hygiene is vital, Stevenson said. Wind down an hour or so before you plan to retire, he suggested. If you can't sleep once you're settled in bed, "don't thrash around for hours. Get up if you can't sleep."

To induce sleep in an unfamiliar environment, Stevenson suggested taking along a "white noise" generator—a machine that emits a mixture of sound waves to mask out unwanted noise interfering with sleep.

Or, take along a personal stereo headset with ocean surf tapes or other repetitive, relaxing sounds, Stevenson said.

He sometimes packs his pillow, which he says is finally broken-in after years of use, but he acknowledges that such accoutrements are not always practical. Light packers might consider toting smaller items, such as a sleep mask to help encourage slumber on the plane or at the destination, he said.

Earplugs can help block out noise. "Try to get a room away from noise", Stevenson suggested. Ask specifically for a room that does not face busy streets and is away from elevators, staircases and ice machines.

Although Stevenson concentrates on the science of sleep, he knows psychology can play a role and is open to remedies that other experts might dismiss.

Does that include the "Awake" and "Asleep" aromatherapy? "Olfactory stimulation can have a very powerful effect on people," he said. "Consider the man who smells perfume and remembers a girlfriend he had 30 years ago.

"Olfactory memory is very strong. If you can find an aroma associated with a very pleasant, very restful situation in which most people would feel sleepy, that could certainly induce sleep."

In the future, some researchers hope, swallowing a pill might make travel-related sleep disruption a problem of the past. Under study is a pill containing a synthetic version of the hormone melatonin, which helps regulate the body's internal clock.

A research team at Oregon Health Sciences University in Portland is now researching its use in humans, said Mary Blood, who is working on the project.

The research is in early stages and the pill is probably years from market, she said. But when her team attended a recent scientific sleep meeting, "there was a lot of interest."

Exercise 3: Read Carefully for Details

Work with a partner. Look in the text for the answers.

1. Describe the contents of the "Revival on arrival" flight kit.

2. How is the aromatherapy used?

3. What problem does aromatherapy try to remedy?

4. Who is affected by jet lag?

5. What are experts studying in order to learn more about travel-related sleep problems?

6. Explain how going into the sun helps get over jet lag.

7. When should you get sun if you fly from east to west?

8. What did the studies of soldiers show about light therapy?

9. What should be avoided to minimize travel-related sleep problems?

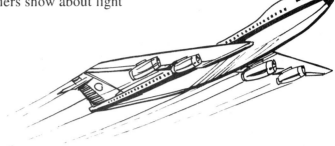

10. How can interaction with people at your destination help you adjust to a new time zone?

11. What is the point to remember about taking sleeping pills?

12. How does Dr. Yudofsky go about prescribing sleeping pills for his patients?

13. Once you are at your destination, what should you do if you can't sleep?

14. List four things that can help you sleep.

15. What does the article say about olfactory stimulation?

16. What might an anti-jet-lag pill in the future contain?

Different Places, Different Customs

Exercise 1: Discuss

Discuss these customs in a group. Which of them would make you feel uncomfortable?

1. someone hugging you when they meet you

2. someone staring at you in the bus

3. someone looking down when they talk to you

4. someone looking at you directly when they talk to you

5. some looking into the distance when you talk to them

6. someone answering their mobile telephone while you are talking to him or her

7. an acquaintance putting his or her arm around you

8. someone you don't know very well kissing you as a greeting

9. someone slapping you on the shoulder when you meet

10. shaking someone's hand when you meet

11. holding a friend's hand as you walk down the street together

12. husbands and wives, or girlfriends and boyfriends, holding hands in public

13. people talking with their hands

14. people sitting or standing close to you

15. someone winking at you

Exercise 2: Use Vocabulary

☐☐ Choose the correct word to complete each space.

Different Places, Different Customs

Anyone who has lived in another culture has had the experience of

misunderstanding some custom or breaking **1**_____ social taboo.
(the, another, some, this)

For instance, think of the custom of the hug. This is a custom some people take

for granted, **2**_____ other people would be shocked if somebody
(if, since, rather, while)

hugged them. In many cultures around the Mediterranean or in South America,

the hug is a **3**_____ and welcoming gesture used to convey
(cold, warm, sad, funny)

acceptance and friendship. Giving or receiving a hug gives people a feeling of

belonging. **4**_____ hugging is not a universal custom. If
(Yet, So, Because, Finally)

someone from a hugging culture hugged a person from a non-hugging culture

such as Britain or China, it could be a social **5**_____ .
(occasion, event, idea, catastrophe)

6_____ custom that has different interpretations in
(Other, Some, Another, Each)

different cultures is eye contact. Some cultures consider looking someone you

meet in the eye to be a **7**_____ of respect and a mark of character.
(sign, bit, lack, idea)

People from these cultures meeting for the first time are sure to look each other in

the eye, shake hands firmly, and speak clearly. **8**_____ is the case
(How, What, Never, This)

in many western cultures. On the other hand, people in many Asian and African

cultures would be **9**_____ to make eye contact with someone
(happy, trying, unlikely, sincere)

they were meeting for the first time. In fact, they would likely avoid eye contact to demonstrate respect. Looking people in the eyes and talking loudly when you met them would probably be seen as quite inappropriate or even **10** _____
(good, polite, bad, rude)
behaviour.

Social distance is something else citizens of the world can't take for granted. How far **11** _____ people sit or stand in a conversation is culturally
(from, apart, near, beside)
determined. All people have a zone of comfort like an invisible circle which

12 _____ people shouldn't enter. The problem is that various
(other, many, another, some)
groups have different ideas about how near is too near. As a result, it is likely that

a Middle Easterner **13** _____ was accustomed to small distances
(which, this, it, who)
between people, and a person from England, who was used to a wide zone of

comfort, would have trouble finding a happy distance **14** _____
(into, during, while, before)
a conversation. The Middle Easterner would probably move forward during

the conversation to feel involved, while the English person would probably

15 _____ back to maintain greater physical distance. Think of the
(touch, write, move, talk)
dance that could result!

Different cultures have different ideas about the subject of touching, too. One

study **16** _____ conducted by a team of sociologists who observed
(is, has, ever, was)
couples talking in restaurants in different cities around the world. They counted the

number of times the couples **17** _____ in the space of an hour.
(touched, smiled, ate, talked)
They found some impressive differences. In London, England, the count was zero.

In Toronto, two contacts per hour **18** _____ recorded. In Paris, the
(was, is, has, were)
couples touched each other an average of 110 times an **19** _____
(day, year, minute, hour)
and in Caracas, Venezuela, the total rose to 180. What a diverse planet we live on.

And how confusing it all is!

Guests and Pests

Listening Activity 9

Exercise 1: Get Ready to Listen

Discuss these questions in a group.

1. How often do people you know visit each other for an afternoon or evening, or for a few days?

2. When you want to visit someone, do you always make arrangements in advance, or do you drop in unannounced?

3. When someone arrives at your doorstep unexpectedly, how do you react?

4. What do you consider a good length of time for a visit?

5. Describe the obligations of a host and of a visitor in your culture.

6. What would you do if a guest overstayed his or her welcome?

7. Do you have a funny story about visiting someone, or about a guest staying at your house? Describe what happened.

Exercise 2: Listen for Meaning

Listen to the information. Which is the main idea?

    a) visiting tourist attractions

    b) why people like to travel

    c) visitors' bad habits

Exercise 3: Listen for Details

Listen to the information. While you listen, answer the questions.

1. Give examples of situations in which a house guest would not be welcome.
2. Give examples of behaviour that is not welcome.
3. What are some things that "slobs" do?
4. Why did the hostess smell smoke when she came home?
5. Explain how a guest's behaviour in the morning can be annoying.
6. Who are sometimes the most difficult guests?
7. What did the aunt do?
8. What did she answer when her niece complained?
9. What did the brother-in-law "help" himself to?
10. What could the brother-in-law have done to make amends?
11. What obligations does a host have?
12. What should a visitor keep in mind?

Visitors

Write about an experience (good or bad) that you have had while visiting, or while having a visitor.

A Tourist Attraction

Exercise 1: Prepare a Report

Prepare a report on a tourist attraction. It can be from the country or province you come from, or from another country that you have visited. Plan to speak for about 15 minutes.

Exercise 2: Present

Present an oral report to the class or your group. Give your audience a chance to ask you questions.

Exercise 3: Write

Write a summary of the information you gave in your report.

Unit 10

At Work

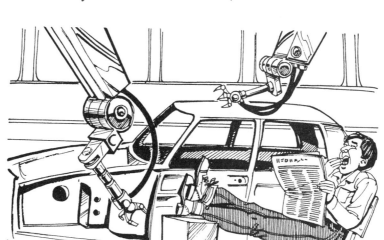

In the Workplace

Exercise 1: Get Ready

What is your ideal job? Perhaps you love chocolate, and dream of working in a chocolate factory. To qualify for such a position, you will need a background in food preparation and a good sense of taste. You will begin work in the quality control lab, where you will monitor and test the chocolate. Your salary will range from about $11 000 to over $60 000 a year if you become a lab director. But whatever your salary or position, you will still get fat if you sample too many of your wares!

Exercise 2: Discuss

Reach a consensus in your group. Rank the following factors in order of importance in determining the quality of your workplace.

a) smoking policy

b) amount of privacy

c) colour of the walls

d) lighting

e) amount of noise

f) reliability of equipment

g) relations with co-workers

h) type of building you work in

Chester Carlson's Marvellous Machine

Listening Activity 10

Exercise 1: Get Ready to Listen

Work in a group. Make a list of machines and equipment that are found in modern offices. Describe how they work and what they do.

Exercise 2: Listen for Meaning

Listen to the information. What machine did Chester Carlson invent?

Exercise 3: Listen for Details

Listen to the information. While you listen, answer the questions.

1. What early invention is one of our most useful devices today?
2. What did Chester Carlson do in his job at the patent office?
3. What kind of books did Carlson read in the library?

4. What was important about sulphur?

5. What was the result of his first experiments?

6. What did he become known for in his neighbourhood?

7. Why did the woman in his building knock on his door?

8. What eventually happened between Carlson and the tenant?

9. What did he and his assistant produce?

10. How did the companies he approached react to Carlson's invention?

11. What deal did he finally make with Haloid?

12. Why was the first machine not very practical?

13. Why were some materials, such as corn meal, rejected?

14. Describe Carlson's problem with paper.

15. What piece of equipment came with the first machine?

16. How much did the first office machine weigh?

17. What problems did the weight of the machine cause?

18. Why did the TV ad show a child operating the machine?

19. How much did the Haloid Company's sales increase in seven years?

Exercise 4: Tell the Story

With a partner, take turns telling the story of Chester Carlson's machine.

Exercise 5: Write the Story

Write everything you remember about Chester Carlson's machine.

Working with People

Exercise 1: Read and Discuss

Read about the following situations. How could the problems be solved?

Situation A

You are having a lot of trouble with a guy you work with. He is a loafer. He often comes in late, and then makes a lot of personal phone calls on office time. He procrastinates, often putting off work on important projects. Then when time gets short, he gets in a panic and asks you to pitch in and help him. You have enough work of your own, and you are tired of helping him out. The boss seems to really like him, though, so if you complain, it only makes you look bad. What can you do?

Situation B

One of your co-workers is a sponger. She's always asking to borrow something. Sometimes it's office supplies, such as your stapler or automatic pencil sharpener. Then, when you need your equipment, you have to go looking for it. When the sponger has a cold, she asks to borrow your box of kleenex. She uses up all the tissues and never replaces the box. But worst of all, she frequently asks to borrow a few bucks until payday. When you ask for the money back a few days later, she acts really annoyed. Sometimes she says she doesn't have the money, and she'll pay you later. What can you do?

Situation C

Your boss is a real tyrant, and everyone is afraid of her. For example, the other day she asked your co-worker for some reports. When your co-worker said he would have them ready the next day, the boss started yelling that she needed the reports right away. The boss is also very grouchy, and gets angry over every little thing. Everyone is afraid to approach her with problems. If you ask for help with something, she says that she is very busy, and that you should not bother her. What can you do?

Situation D

You work with someone who is very nice, but there's just one problem. That person is a gossip. During coffee breaks in the cafeteria, he is always very friendly and asks lots of questions. The next thing you know, you hear personal information being repeated by others. It's very hard to avoid him because you work together. Sometimes, when you get a personal phone call at work, you notice that he seems to be listening to your conversations. What can you do? You don't like your personal life to be the subject of conversation at the water cooler.

Situation E

Your co-worker is a workaholic. Every morning when you come in to work, she's already at her desk. When you leave at 5:00, she's still sitting there, working away. Sometimes she doesn't even take a coffee break, or go out for lunch with the rest of the gang. Whenever the boss needs some extra help, this eager beaver volunteers to do the work. The problem is that she makes everyone else look bad when they work normal hours. What can you do?

Situation F

You depend on a photocopy machine to do your job. Frequently, when you go to the photocopy room, all three machines are down. Sometimes the machines are out of paper. Sometimes there are paper jams that haven't been cleared. Sometimes there is some mechanical or electrical problem. Whenever you ask someone for help, that person says: "It's not my job to take care of the machines." You have had enough of these shirkers. Someone has to take responsibility. What is the solution?

Exercise 2: Review Vocabulary

Work with a partner. Match the personality type with the expression. Find the best answers for each.

1. the shirker   I'll try to get to it next week.

2. the grouch   Can I borrow a few bucks till payday?

3. the sponger   That's not my job.

4. the gossip   Isn't it time for a coffee break?

5. the eager beaver   I need those reports, and I need them now!

6. the workaholic   Did you hear about…?

7. the loafer   I'll be in on the weekend to work.

8. the tyrant   Leave me alone. I'm busy.

9. the procrastinator   Here, let me do that!

Did You Know?   People often watch the clock as they work, waiting for their coffee break or quitting time. When Thomas Alva Edison opened his first manufacturing plant, he was annoyed by this habit, and decided to solve the problem. He installed dozens of clocks in the factory, each set to a different time. Because no one knew the exact time any more, people stopped looking at the clocks and concentrated on their work!

The Robotics Revolution

Video Activity 3: Part 1

Exercise 1: Get Ready to Watch the Video

Discuss these questions in a group.

1. What are some working conditions that are generally considered to be unpleasant or undesirable?

2. List some dangerous, boring, or repetitive jobs you would not like to have.

3. What are some problems that could result if many jobs currently done by human beings were done by robots?

4. Name some places where robots are used today.

5. Where do you think robots may be used in the future?

Exercise 2: Watch the Video for General Ideas

Watch the video. Then work in a group to list six facts you learned from watching the video.

Exercise 3: Watch the Video for Details

While you watch the video, answer the questions. Use the worksheet.

1. Where does the word "robot" come from?
2. Name three things the robot Wasubot can do.
3. What song does Wasubot play?
4. Name three places where robots are already found today, and one place they may be found tomorrow.
5. What job were tele-operators designed to do?
6. What was the limitation of tele-operators?
7. What kind of a machine did scientists dream of?
8. In what areas of robotics does Japan lead the world?
9. Describe show robots.
10. What features does Fanuc man have?
11. How does Fanuc man embody the definition of a robot?
12. What problem could a robot have in imitating the actions of the human hand?
13. How have scientists overcome the problem?
14. What do the robots build at night?
15. What characteristics interest the makers of industrial robots?
16. What would the ideal computer brain have?
17. What does the field of artificial intelligence seek to do?

Night Work

Exercise 1: Get Ready to Read

Work in a group. Read these statements about working at night. Discuss whether each is true (**T**) or false (**F**).

1. About 20 percent of full-time workers in North America work at night.
2. In the future fewer people will work at night.
3. People's bodies adjust if they work at night over a long period.
4. All of these people might be at work during the night: nurses, bankers, journalists, stockbrokers.
5. It is more economical for factories to stay open all night.
6. Night workers lose one night's sleep every week.
7. Night workers drink and smoke less than day workers.
8. Falling asleep is a common problem for night workers.

📖 Exercise 2: Read Quickly to Check Predictions

Read the text quickly. Check your answers to the true/false questions in Exercise 1.

Night Work

Sandy Bauers

Knight-Ridder Newspapers

It was 3 a.m. and Milton Hay barely had a moment to chat. While the rest of the world slept peacefully and dreamed sweetly—or so it seemed—Hay was churning out photocopies. He does that all night long. Fridays through Mondays.

He was hardly the only one awake. Milton Hay is just one of 20 million night workers in North America—almost 20 percent of the full-time work force. They not only police our streets, tend our sick and keep our electricity humming, they also transport our goods, monitor our money, entertain us on TV and will sell us a dozen eggs.

Everything seems to be moving to 24-hour mode, from convenience stores to massage parlours. Not even clerical workers go home at 5 p.m. any more. In many cities, support staff at large firms work well into the night. Economists predict the number of people who work "non-standard" schedules will continue to grow as advances in technology link the globe's time zones.

Never mind that night work is bad for your health. Sleep clinics, staffed by yet another group of night workers, have found that even those who have worked nights for years may never get used to it. Their body clocks can't adjust.

Just ask journalist Kevin Coyne. Intrigued by an odd statistic he came across—that at 3 a.m. on any given night, 10 million people in the United States were awake— he decided to look into it.

Most daysiders are unaware of the extent of night work. "If I tell people I work nights, they assume I'm a nurse", a bank employee in Boston told Coyne. Passing the city's big office building at night "they think someone just left the lights on."

Business sees the night as a natural resource—the only one we can't deplete. Tapping the wee hours has spawned a new industry—overnight mail—and altered the financial world. It makes economic sense for a business with expensive equipment to expand operating hours, says a labour economist. Why shell out for the equipment, then let it sit idle for two-thirds of the day? For the price of one operator you can keep a bank of machines whirring all night.

But they are tired. Night workers lose, on average, a full night's worth of sleep every week. Milton Hay, who has a full-time day job as well, says he sleeps only three hours out of every 24—from 7 to 10 p.m. And he manages without coffee. Others are not so lucky. As a group, night workers use more caffeine and other stimulants, drink more alcohol, take more sleeping pills. Everything is magnified if you work a changing shift.

And more than 70 percent of night workers admit they fall asleep on the job every night. Which brings up the issues of job performance and safety. If a trucker zipping along at 60 miles an hour or a nuclear power plant operator goes to sleep for even a minute, the results can be deadly.

Yet night work remains largely unstudied. Not even the health effects have been documented. In addition to specific health problems, researchers are concerned about "shift work maladaptation syndrome": a fancy way of saying that people on shift work "feel lousy all the time." You're asking your body to sleep when it wants to be awake, and to stay awake when it wants to sleep. It's similar to jet lag, only it's constant.

Some people want to work the night shift, though. Coyne says it is common in two-career couples with limited child-care options. Some workers say they like the illusion of added time—they can get more chores done during the day. Some are avid golfers. Many enjoy free city parking at night and like not having to buck rush-hour traffic. Few do it for the money, because often there's not enough financial incentive to turn one's life upside down.

By the end of his journey, Coyne developed an affinity for the night time. He found that people were friendlier. They had a healthy disdain for authority and "a willingness to endure adversity." People who work at night, he says "tend to think deeper", because there are fewer distractions. "They have more room and space and freedom to think."

On the other hand, Marty Klein, a psychologist who runs a shift-work consulting firm, imagines life without "medical coverage, police, telephone, television, radio, heat, light, water. If we didn't have shift work we'd live from 5 p.m. to 8 a.m. without any of that. Weekends would not be fun. Weekends would be anarchy.

"It's really these people," Klein says, "that make the difference between our modern culture, for all of its pros and cons, vs. literally the dark ages."

Exercise 3: Read Carefully for Details

Work with a partner. Look in the text for the answers.

1. What kind of work does Milton Hay do?

2. Name five jobs that people do at night.

3. Why do economists predict that the number of night-time jobs will grow in the future?

4. Why do researchers say that working nights is bad for the health?

5. How many people in the United States are awake in the middle of the night?

6. How do businesses view the night?

7. Why does it make economic sense for businesses to operate at night?

8. How much sleep do night workers lose?

9. What do many night workers take to manage their lifestyle?

10. Give some examples of situations in which disasters can occur if a person falls asleep on the job.

11. Why do many night workers "feel lousy all the time"?

12. Give three reasons why some people like to work at night.

13. What are some characteristics of people who work at night?

14. What services would we not have, if people did not work the night shift?

The Robotics Revolution

Video Activity 3: Part 2

Exercise 1: Get Ready to Watch the Video

Work in a group. Without looking back to Part 1, list everything you can remember about how robots are used.

Exercise 2: Watch the Video for General Ideas

Watch the video. Then work in a group to give information about how robots are used:

    a) in hospitals

    b) in department stores

    c) in factories

    d) in schools

Sign in a bank in Coquitlam, BC:

Due to a shortage of robots, some of our workers are human and may act unpredictably when abused.

Exercise 3: Watch the Video for Details

Watch the video. While you watch, answer the questions. Use the worksheet.

1. How is the robot at Vancouver General Hospital used?
2. What task would be difficult for the surgical team without the use of Arthrobot?
3. What two techniques are used to control Arthrobot?
4. Name some possible future medical uses of robots.
5. For what kind of job demands are robots ideal?
6. Explain why the semi-conductor industry likes to use robot arms.
7. Give details of the "robotic system" in the department store.
8. Name two future jobs for which rolling robots may be used.
9. What ability does a robot need in order to move on uneven ground?
10. Explain how a robot can climb stairs.
11. How does the robot see?
12. Why do the Seiko Watch factory robots need vision?
13. Give statistics about the increase in the use of robots in Japan and the United States.
14. Why will robots never eliminate the need for people in the workplace?
15. What will be necessary if people are to be ready to meet the demands of the robotic revolution?
16. What conclusion does the video reach?

Exercise 4: Write

Discuss some ways robots would be useful for boring and repetitive jobs in the home. What aspects of the robot technology described in the video would be useful?

Unit 11

Family Ties

For Better or For Worse

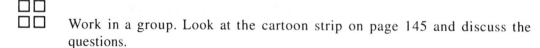

Listening Activity 11

Interview with Lynn Johnston, Cartoonist

Exercise 1: Get Ready to Listen

Work in a group. Look at the cartoon strip on page 145 and discuss the questions.

1. How old is the boy?
2. To whom do you think he is talking?
3. What is the message in the cartoon strip?
4. Could this situation happen in your family?
5. Can you identify with either of the people in the comic strip? Explain why.
6. What subjects do you not talk about with members of your family?
7. How much privacy is it reasonable to expect within a family?

Exercise 2: Listen for Meaning

While you listen, close your book. After you listen, work in a group and see if you can list five facts about Lynn Johnston.

Exercise 3: Listen for Details

Listen to the interview. While you listen, answer the questions.

1. Why did Lynn first begin drawing cartoons?
2. Why did she choose the family as a focus?
3. What emotions does she mention in relation to her family?
4. What was her experience of breaking into the cartoon business?
5. How long has Lynn had a cartoon strip in the papers?
6. Why do the people in her cartoon strip look like people in her family?
7. How did she feel when she signed her first contract and why?
8. Are the stories she writes today based on her family's experiences?
9. According to Lynn, what are the concerns of teenagers such as her daughter?
10. What are some of the difficulties faced by people who have both old parents and teenage children?
11. Name some countries where For Better or For Worse appears.
12. Why is translation of cartoons a problem?

Did You Know?   The words "to love and to cherish, in sickness and in health, for richer or for poorer, for better or for worse…" come from the wedding ceremony.

Exercise 4: Tell the Story

☐☐ Work with a partner. Take turns telling each other what you can remember about the interview with Lynn Johnston.

Exercise 5: Write

Write what you can remember about the interview with Lynn Johnston.

The Pecking Order

☐☐ Choose the correct auxiliary verb for each space.

are   will   may   have   is   can   might   were

You _____ think that all chickens are equal, but scientists who study animal
        1

behaviour tell us that this is not always so. By watching the interaction

between chickens in a barnyard, zoologists _____ been able to observe that
                                            2

the biggest chicken often likes to show who is boss by pecking the chicken

next to it. That chicken _____ then peck a smaller, weaker chicken, and so
                          3

on. Soon all the chickens will have a place in the hierarchy. This hierarchy

_____ called the pecking order.
4

In human families, things are a little different, but anthropologists and

psychologists who study human behaviour say that they _____ also observe
                                                       5

characteristics related to hierarchy. They feel that the characteristics that any

of us has _____ determined by the place we occupy in the family pecking
           6

order. In other words, whether people grow up assertive, easy going, tense, or

conciliatory _____ have a lot to do with the position they had while they
              7

_____ growing up.
8

A Place in the Family

Exercise 1 : Get Ready to Read

Discuss these questions in a group.

1. What is the size of the family in which you grew up?
2. What position did you have in the family (oldest, youngest, etc.)?
3. Is there anything that you didn't like about your position in the family when you were growing up?
4. Were there any advantages to the position you had in the family?
5. What do you think is the most desirable place in the family?

Exercise 2: Read Quickly for General Ideas

Read the text quickly. Find the paragraphs that talk about:

1. first-born children
2. only children
3. middle children
4. last-born children

A Place in the Family

A. None of us chooses the kind of family into which we will be born. It may be a big family, a small family, or somewhere in-between. There may be brothers, sisters, a mixture of siblings, or we may be only children. Each of us has a place in the family hierarchy, however, and each of us strives to fit into the family in our own way. According to some experts, our birth order may determine many of the personality traits we develop later in life.

B. Think about the youngest or last-born child. People often describe the baby of the family as spoiled and demanding. The exception, of course, is last-borns themselves, who may be more inclined to describe themselves as victims of their bossy, know-it-all elders. Anthropologists who study the family point to the relaxed, outgoing nature of youngest children. They suggest that they grow up competing with older children for their parents' attention and learn to be natural entertainers. One advantage of being the last to arrive in the family is that the parents have often eased up on many of the rules and regulations that governed older children. With parents paying less attention, last-born children are free to follow their own dreams without interference.

C. One study of birth order found that three-quarters of the major scientific inventions made in the last five years can be attributed to youngest children. The study points out that the career choices of last-borns reflect their relaxed, people-oriented approach to life. They will often be found in fields that employ their optimistic, creative, fun-loving approach to life. Consequently, last-borns may often choose to work in sales, entertainment, science, or helping professions such as therapy, nursing, and social work.

D. First-born children, as a group, display another set of characteristics. As the first child on the scene, a first-born meets with inexperienced parents and becomes the guinea pig for all of the parents' good intentions. By comparison, later-born children have the benefit of more experienced, relaxed parents. By the time later babies are born, parents have more realistic and reasonable expectations for their children.

E. At the same time, first-borns benefit from having their parents' undivided attention. Higher expectations are communicated to them and they are groomed for success. However, they may suffer the disadvantage of having to set a good example for younger children. Older children are often given a lot of responsibility early on, and expected to make decisions for younger siblings.

F. One of the characteristics that scientists attribute to family position is a more dominant and confident nature in first-borns. These children have been trained to assume responsibility readily, and they make good leaders. Other traits that have been observed in first-borns are self-confidence and generosity. Oldest children are also good listeners. Because they are serious and goal-oriented, they are often found in professions such as architecture, journalism, teaching, and law. All the astronauts chosen for the US space programmes have been first-borns.

G. What about middle children? Sandwiched between older and younger siblings, they can feel like the forgotten ones in the family. Middle children are often observed to be the most secretive members of the family. Their characteristics can be hard to pin down. This is not surprising when you consider that a middle child may be the second of three, or the third of six, for example. In addition, middle children may be second children, but still be the first girl or the first boy in the family.

H. People studying birth positions have noted that middle children tend to be better adjusted than their brothers and sisters. They are often good problem solvers and they display good skills as negotiators. Middle-borns are generally noted for their tact, loyalty, and humour. Being natural negotiators, they frequently find careers as managers, counsellors, and diplomats, and may have high ambitions that allow them to surpass their older siblings.

I. Finally, there are only children. Like first-borns, they are initiators and leaders. Because their parents have had such high hopes for them, they tend to have high standards for themselves. Only children are often serious and scholarly, and they are attracted to the same careers as first-borns. Like first-borns, they enjoy taking initiative; but unlike first-borns, they may not get along well with people their own age. They may be better at dealing with older people and younger children, in relationships where their roles are clearly defined.

J. Are the experts telling us that our place in the family will determine our character traits for life? No, not really. What experts do say is that, while birth order may influence the kind of people we become, in the long run many other life experiences play as great a role. In the final analysis, the way we are is really up to us.

Exercise 3: Read Carefully for Details

Work with a partner. Look in the text for the answers.

1. What do some experts believe about our personality traits?

2. How is the baby of the family sometimes described?

3. How does the last-born sometimes answer?

4. According to anthropologists, why do last-borns seem to be natural entertainers?

5. Why are last-borns often freer than older children to follow their dreams?

6. What careers do last-borns often choose and why?

7. What problem do first-born children have with their parents?

8. What advantage do later-born children have?

9. Why are first-born children frequently successful in their careers?

10. Why do first-borns make good leaders?

11. What professions attract oldest children?

12. Why are the characteristics of middle children more difficult to observe?

13. List some traits of middle children.

14. Why do only children have high standards for themselves?

15. Name one difference between first and only children.

16. Do experts believe that our place in the family determines our characteristics for life? Explain.

Exercise 4: Practise Vocabulary

Work with a partner. Match the meanings.

1.	characteristics	define
2.	brothers and sisters	show
3.	benefit	try
4.	pecking order	hopes
5.	people oriented	place
6.	expectations	traits
7.	pin down	outgoing
8.	strive	siblings
9.	eased up	hierarchy
10.	determine	relaxed
11.	display	advantage
12.	position	influence

Exercise 5: Write

Write about your place in the family and how you think it affected your character.

Family Feuds

Exercise 1: Read and Discuss

Work in a group. Read about some family situations. After each paragraph, discuss solutions to the problems.

A. I just got married. I love my husband very much, but I don't know if I can live with him much longer. The problem is that he snores—really loudly. He sounds like a buzz saw. He keeps me awake half the night, and then I walk around exhausted all day long. I've tried shaking him, but that doesn't work. He stops for a moment, then rolls over and starts again. We don't have any extra bedrooms in our house, so I can't go to another room to sleep. I asked him to see a doctor, to check if he has a medical problem. He just laughed, and says I must be imagining it—he doesn't snore at all! What should I do?

B. My sister-in-law and I were both expecting our first babies around the same time. Naturally, we were both thrilled about our babies, and about having the cousins grow up at the same time. Then I mentioned that, if I had a boy, I was planning to name him Charlie after my father. My sister-in-law said: "That's funny! We were planning to name our baby Charlie, if it's a boy." We all laughed about it at the time. Then her baby was born two weeks before mine, and she named him Charlie! At first, I thought it would be cute to have the two babies with the same names. But when my son was born, I realized it was not a good idea. I had no name picked out for my son, and I was furious that she had stolen my baby's name. For three days my child had no name. Then I settled for "Ben," which I don't like nearly as much. Now I get so upset when I see her "Charlie," that I can hardly speak to her anymore. What should I do?

C. My problem is my brother, who has recently become a vegetarian. Now, I can understand his feelings, and I even agree with his sentiments. The problem is that he expects everyone to change to his way of thinking. For example, last week I invited him and his wife over for a family dinner. I served meat as the main course, because my husband and children like it. But I also served several vegetarian dishes. Well, my brother didn't appreciate my efforts at all. He kept complaining about why I was serving meat, and why everyone wasn't vegetarian like he is. He and his wife refused to eat the vegetable dishes I prepared because they were made in the same oven as the meat! The only things they would eat were dessert and coffee. Boy, was I annoyed. I used to be very close to my brother, but this is tearing us apart. What can I do?

D. My problem is my aunt, who comes to visit once a year. She's a very sweet person, except in one respect. She's a snoop. As soon as I leave the house to go to work, she starts looking through my personal belongings. She says that she knows I'm very busy, and she is just trying to help me organize my things. On the last visit, she rearranged the contents of all my drawers and cupboards! I know they were a little messy, but at least I knew where everything was. Now I can't find anything. I really resent her snooping through my private things, but if I say anything about it, she's very offended. She is my only aunt, and I really love her, but I can't take this any more. What can I do? How can I get her to mind her own business?

E. My problem is my brother-in-law. He loves to eat, especially at our house. Whenever he comes over, he heads straight for the refrigerator, and starts eating everything in sight. Last weekend he dropped by, and ate half a chicken that I was saving for dinner. Then he polished off the rest of the chocolate cake and drank all the milk. When I asked him not to touch the pie I had baked for a friend's party, he acted really hurt. He's a single guy, so he probably doesn't realize how much it costs to feed a family. Help! How can I stop him from eating us out of house and home?

Exercise 2: Discuss and Write

Work in a group. Think of a family problem and write about it. Describe the problem in as much detail as you can.

Did You Know?   A nuclear family is made up of parents and their children. An extended family includes parents, children, grandparents, and/or uncles and aunts in the same household.

Family Lies

Exercise 1: Get Ready to Read

Discuss these questions in a group.

1. Describe an ideal family that you know personally.
2. Do you think that relations between parents and children were better or worse in the past?
3. Do you think that family life is better in other parts of the world than in North America?
4. Why do you think that divorce is so common in North America today?
5. What do you think is the ideal age for two people to marry? Discuss why.
6. What do you think is the ideal number of children? Give reasons for your answer.

Exercise 2: Read Quickly for General Ideas

Read the article. Which of these is the main idea?

a) changes in the family throughout history

b) how to find a husband or wife

c) families in the future

Family Lies

Marsha Skuce

Ottawa Citizen

You think divorce rates spell the end of the family? Well, a couple of centuries ago the average marriage lasted 12 years. You think working mothers are unravelling the very fabric of hearth and home? The truth is that, except for a few decades in this century, women have always worked. You think the family is in crisis? "Every age thinks the family is in crisis," says historian Chad Gaffield of the University of Ottawa. "The Greeks and Romans wrung their hands about loutish youth, too."

But the current sense of crisis, says Gaffield, comes from the mistaken belief we are losing the ideal family—husband and wife sharing years of wedded bliss; a multitude of loving children; and several generations living together in harmonious support. It was never thus.

154

Arranged Marriages

In traditional European society—from about 1450 to 1700—marriage, he says "had nothing to do with love and romance." Romeo and Juliette could only happen on the stage.

In real life, teenagers married if their families arranged it—and then, only among the aristocracy, for whom marriages were usually politically strategic. Ordinary people married much later in life. Couples had to wait until they could support a household. In agrarian Europe with well-settled farms, that meant waiting until someone, usually a parent, died and got off the land.

Mom did not stay home and look after the kids. Mom and Dad and the kids worked, on the farm or looking after the shoemaking shop. Children were raised, says Gaffield in a "looser, more community-centred environment, in the street."

The view that yesterday's children were better disciplined and more respectful of their elders probably isn't true, Gaffield says. The evidence is that there was an enormous amount of alienation between generations. Children waiting for an economic foothold to start their lives put pressure on parents. And parents were suspicious. For example, formalized, legal arrangements in which children promised specific amounts of food and lodging space for dependant parents were not uncommon.

Family Size

Limiting family size for various reasons has always been part of domestic life, says Gaffield. For example, birth control was practised widely in Italian city-states of the 14th century. The aristocratic families who ruled them wanted heirs of course, but were terrified of more than one. "One son ensured political continuity: too many sons meant competition, division, maybe the breakup of power."

The family began to change with the discovery of the New World. "All of a sudden, there was land," says Gaffield. The industrial revolution brought changes too. In an expanding economy people didn't have to sit around and wait for Dad to die, they could get jobs. And their lives changed. In the 1700s

and the first half of the 19th century, the average marriage age dropped to the mid-20s. Family size grew to an average of seven children.

In Canada and the United States and Europe, the general fertility began declining by the 1850s. By the 1920s, the average family size had dropped to three to four children. And with the 60s and the Pill, it dropped even further.

People began asking, "How many do we need to support us in our old age?" The family as an all purpose institution was changing. "The days of the home as life's centre stage—a place for birth, education, work — were dying," Gaffield says. "Now you were born in a hospital, learned in a school, worked in an office or factory."

The Ideal Marriage

Marriage itself was seen in a new light. Free to marry earlier and living longer lives, people began to see marriage as more than an economic union. "I think they began to say, 'Holy mackerel, I'm going to be with this person for 20, maybe 30 years.' And they started looking for quality in the arrangement." The foundation of marriage came to be seen as emotional. Divorce rates, Gaffield maintains, may be a reflection of unrealistically high expectations that place "an enormous burden" on emotions. Unlike those of earlier days, marriages now "are being asked to go on and on."

Did that ideal family we've come to believe is the norm ever exist? Gaffield says probably yes. For one brief historical moment—from the 1920s to the 1950s. Built on an economy that allowed a family to get by, even thrive, on one pay cheque, the first half of the 20th century set up the supposed ideal: Father at work, Mother at home with the two children.

Exercise 3: Read Carefully for Details

Work with a partner. Look in the text for the answers.

1. What three beliefs does Chad Gaffield refer to in the opening paragraph?

2. What is the mistaken belief he refers to?

3. How is the ideal family defined?

4. Why did the story of Romeo and Juliette not represent reality at that time?

5. Why did many people have to wait a long time before they married in the past?

6. Give an example to show that there was "an enormous amount of alienation between generations."

7. Why was birth control widely practised by aristocratic families in fourteenth-century Italian states?

8. What two developments brought changes to the size of families in the eighteenth century?

9. What was the size of the average family by the 1920s?

10. What contributed to the decline in family size in the 1960s?

11. Compare the role of the family in the past and today.

12. Why did people begin to see marriage as more than an economic union?

13. What does Gaffield think might be the cause of the high divorce rates we see today?

14. When did the supposed ideal family exist in reality?

15. Describe roles in the family in the early twentieth century.

Exercise 4: Review Vocabulary

Find these expressions in the text. Choose the best synonyms for the words that are bold.

1. **spell** the end
   a) count
   b) write
   c) cause
   d) cancel

2. **unravelling** the very fabric of hearth and home
   a) improving
   b) destroying
   c) supporting
   d) watching

3. wrung their hands about **loutish** youth
   a) happy
   b) friendly
   c) rude
   d) serious

4. sharing years of wedded **bliss**
   a) difficulties
   b) problems
   c) conflict
   d) happiness

5. could only happen **on the stage**
   a) in reality
   b) on the street
   c) in the theatre
   d) by accident

6. waiting for an **economic foothold**
   a) support
   b) bandage
   c) miracle
   d) game

7. they wanted **heirs**
   a) power
   b) money
   c) children
   d) property

8. ensure political **continuity**
   a) future
   b) power
   c) alliances
   d) support

9. the average marriage age **dropped**
   a) increased
   b) decreased
   c) went up
   d) changed

10. to **support** us in our old age
    a) drop
    b) count on
    c) look after
    d) advise

11. an enormous **burden**
    a) strength
    b) growth
    c) weight
    d) event

12. even **thrive**
    a) expand
    b) spend
    c) transfer
    d) prosper

Did You Know?   One prediction for the future of the family is that family size won't change. It will stay at two children. Marriage will change, however, with people marrying two or three times over a lifetime.

Unit 12

Money Madness

Money Makes the World Go Around
Discussion
Reading
Vocabulary

Credit Cards
Vocabulary
Cultural Information

Who's in Charge?
Listening Activity 12

Lying, Cheating, and Stealing
Interaction

Two Sides of the Coin
Discussion

Money Makes the World Go Around

Exercise 1: Get Ready to Read

Discuss these questions in a group.

1. How much money do you need to be happy?

2. How much money does someone need to be rich?

3. If you had an unlimited amount of money, how would you spend it?

4. Do you consider yourself to be "cheap," reasonable, or a spendthrift?

5. Do you think your spending habits are similar to those of your parents, or different?

6. What is the relationship between money and happiness?

Exercise 2: Read for Information

Scan the text on the following pages. Look for the answers to these questions.

1. What are the top three expenditures by the average Canadian family?

2. Compare the rate at which Canadians save money with that at which Americans save.

3. Compare the number of savings accounts with the number of people in Canada.

4. On what do Canadians spend 2.5 billion annually?

5. What was the value of life insurance owned by Canadians in 1984?

6. What are shinplasters?

7. According to Canada's Currency and Exchange Act, what is the largest debt that can be paid exclusively in coins?

8. How much money did the Johnson family of Toronto put into circulation? How?

9. What does Section 415 of the Criminal Code prohibit?

10. What do Americans often think of Canadian currency?

11. What does EFT/POS stand for?

12. How does a debit card work?

Money Makes the World Go Around

Royal Bank Reporter

Get-rich-quick schemes are a dime a dozen. And some of them are even legal: discover a gold mine, crack the lottery system, follow the advice of D. Moneybag's investment newsletter, sell cosmetics door to door, marry a millionaire, become a movie star or television faith healer, invent a new computer chip or a better mousetrap. Someone somewhere has struck it rich on such ventures—and then, naturally, written a best-seller about how ordinary folks can do the same. Good luck! But don't hold your breath.

"Everyone wants to make money, but how many want it enough to work for it?" The crotchety question once asked by Canadian newspaper tycoon Roy Thompson was answered in part by Robert Zend, a Toronto author: "I am willing to do anything for money, even work." For most of us, income means money made from earnings. Many breadwinners will earn a couple of million dollars during their lifetime. However, lifelong earnings look considerably more on paper than they are once taxes, inflation, and costs of living have taken their inevitable cuts.

On the other hand, one dinky dollar can grow into a multitude of dollars if it is saved and invested. A single dollar annually compounded at a 10 percent rate of interest will grow to $45.26 in 40 years. A $10 investment increases to $452.60 over the same period. $100 to $4526. $1000 to $45 260. And so on and so forth. The trick is to start saving money as early as possible to reap the windfall in the future.

Where Our Money Goes

The three top expenditures by an average Canadian family are—in order—personal taxes, shelter, and food. Transportation is the next largest outlay, followed by clothing, recreation, and household operation costs.

And what do we do with the money that's left over? We put it primarily in RRSPs, term deposits, savings accounts and Canada Savings Bonds, which together account for about 80 percent of the money Canadians invest. The remaining goes into such investments as real estate (other than the home) and stocks.

Canadians save money at twice the rate of Americans, who currently owe $4.7 billion in credit-card debt alone and rank far below their counterparts in other industrialized countries as savers. In Canada, though, personal-savings accounts outnumber the people in the country by five million.

Though Canadians may appear financially conservative, we do shell out some $2.5 billion annually for lottery tickets. And while fewer than 10 percent of us participate in the stock market, seven billion shares with a value of $58 billion were traded on Canadian stock exchanges in 1985. But that's chicken feed compared with the $679 billion Canadians owned in life insurance in 1984. For a guaranteed return, individual Canadians also agree to lend the federal government large sums of money every year in the form of Canada Savings Bonds, which we bought to the tune of $15.1 billion in 1985.

Unique Canadian Money

Although Canadian currency is a Johnny-come-lately on the world monetary scene, three of our coins and paper notes are unique in the colourful annals of international money.

• Playing card money, Canada's first paper money, was issued in New France in 1685 and remained in circulation for a total of 64 years. This peculiar government note was a child of necessity: when coin-bearing ships failed to arrive in Quebec on time, authorities cut playing cards into quarters, to which they affixed an official seal and the governor's signature.

• Shinplasters were 25-cent government notes introduced in 1870. Like playing card money, shinplasters were issued as a stop-gap measure (in this instance, to counteract the flood of American coins in Canada); but the notes lived on until 1935, when the newly founded Bank of Canada recalled the popular currency. Shinplasters probably derived their name from a similar kind of bill soldiers used to pad their boots during the American Revolution.

Hard Cash Has its Limits

In 1986 Gary Shave, a 28-year-old sandblaster and painter with a Port Tobinson, Ontario, company, asked his former employer for the $941 he was owed in back pay. The boss obliged by paying him off in buckets full of pennies, nickels, and dimes. Although Shave accepted the cumbersome settlement, he didn't have to. According to Canada's Currency and Exchange Act, only a debt of up to $10 can be paid exclusively in coins, providing that the coins are not less in value than a 10-cent piece. A debt of up to $5, however, can be paid in nickels. The maximum limit for paying a debt in pennies alone is 25 cents.

Funny Money (I)

Many families band together to make money, and back in the 1880s, the Johnson family of Toronto was no exception. Their joint financial enterprise was, however, rather offbeat: they made money themselves—literally. Papa Johnson engraved counterfeit plates for bank notes, on which his daughters forged bank officials' signatures and which his sons then printed. Mama Johnson in turn sold the bogus notes to a wholesale money dealer. By the time the famous private detective John Wilson Murray caught the crooks, the all-in-the family operation had put more than $1 million into circulation.

Be warned: Section 415 of the Criminal Code prohibits the illustration, photographing, or reproducing of the likeness or appearance of all or part of a current bank note and, of course, its counterfeiting.

Funny Money (II)

Parker Brothers issued $2 699 931 340 in Canada in 1985—nearly $2 billion more than the Bank of Canada put into circulation. But this particular money operation is altogether legal because Parker Brothers' output is of use only in the company's Monopoly games.

Americans often think of Canada's colourful currency as some kind of funny play money, even though our bills are much more difficult to counterfeit and much easier to distinguish from one another than their uniform greenbacks. Asked one American guest at Expo '86 in Vancouver: "Is this Canadian money good off-site?"

Still, crazy Canuck moolah has a new-found appeal to practical Yankees. "Could you ask for a friendlier, more accommodating currency?" an American travel magazine asked its readers. "As you mope over the sad state of the dollar in Europe and Japan, you can rejoice in the 30 percent discount on your hotel room, restaurant bill, and even the toothbrush you bought to replace the one you forgot."

Is there Cash in our Future?

A cash-free society has been speculated about since the dawning of the age of electronics. At a 1986 conference of retailers and bankers in Toronto, no one came out and predicted that a cashless society loomed in the immediate future; however, one speaker clearly foresaw a "less-cash" society.

He might be right: the advent of a debit card, an offspring of the automated teller card and grandchild of the credit card, is now being tested in Saskatchewan and Ontario. Recent studies predict that within a decade one-third of the sales at Canadian retail stores will be paid for by the debit card, which is officially known as Electronic Funds Transfer/Point of Sale, or EFT/POS for short; within a generation, debit cards may well be the standard way to purchase consumer goods. Here's how the debit card works: a customer presents the card, which is passed through a card reader and then keyed into a personal identification number. In a matter of seconds, the customer's account is debited for the amount of the purchase, and a printer provides a receipt.

Just as people once overcame their resistance to paper money, many of us now have come to accept the notion of electronic money. Dr. Lambert Gardiner, a Montreal psychologist and futures theorist, regards the high-tech debit card as a potential boon to individual money management. "EFT can assist us in seeing our financial status more concretely, and this will enable us to have a more perceptive grasp of things," he was quoted as saying in a recent issue of *Your Money* magazine that focused on Canada's "new banking." "In the Information Age, money is a blip on a screen," Dr. Gardiner continued. "In one eye-gulp this information is transformed into knowledge, and this knowledge helps us to reduce the uncertainties in our lives."

Inevitably, electronic money will become more and more of a reality in our daily lives. But don't start putting aside your metal coins and paper currency as collectors' items just yet. Ready money will remain a trustworthy partner for a long time to come.

Exercise 3: Review Vocabulary

Match the words on the left to the definitions on the right.

1.	a fine	weekly or monthly payments from an employer
2.	a bribe	a tax on imports
3.	duty	pocket money that parents give children
4.	a tip	one dollar
5.	allowance	money paid for education
6.	tuition	money paid for transportation
7.	wages	money that you borrow
8.	a grand	extra money (often 15 percent) given for good service in a restaurant
9.	a loan	an hourly rate of pay from an employer
10.	fare	an under-the-table payment to an official
11.	salary	money you pay if you break the law
12.	a buck	one thousand dollars

Credit Cards

☐☐ Read the paragraphs. Choose the best word to complete each sentence.

Credit cards are a relatively new idea. The concept of "buy now, pay later" was

1 _____ in 1950 when a businessman in New York
(discovered, conceived, cancelled, changed)

was dining in a restaurant and had an **2** _____
(funny, exciting, dangerous, embarrassing)

experience. When the **3** _____ brought his check, the
(experience, server, restaurant, meal)

man realized that he didn't have enough money with him to pay for his meal. This

experience gave him an idea that led to the first credit card. The "Diner's Club" was

born when the **4** _____ convinced 28 clubs and
(waiter, banker, cook, businessman)

restaurants to accept a plastic card instead of cash.

By the 1960s, credit cards were being mailed **5** _____
(daily, unsolicited, registered, weekly)

to almost any adult who had a name and address. The crisp, clean plastic of the

cards became popular very quickly. The power of the small plastic cards to

6 _____ what had been unattainable wishes became a
(change, persuade, gratify, create)

national obsession, as people discovered that they could begin buying and

consuming merely by **7** _____ their names. Using a credit
(signing, changing, printing, giving)

card made it possible to buy a sweater in Halifax or a washing machine in

Edmonton without **8** _____ twice. A new era was born.
(paying, signing, buying, thinking)

Today credit cards are such an important feature of our way of doing business

that you may even have trouble **9** _____ a hotel room or
(finding, deciding, booking, paying)

renting a car without one. Credit cards also make impulse buying easy.

10 _____ , if you suddenly need a vacation, a
(However, For example, Nevertheless, In addition)

new outfit, or a meal in a good restaurant, a credit card gives you the power to buy

now and pay **11** _____ . There is no doubt that credit cards make it
(later, less, weekly, more)

simple to experience the thrill of acquisition, and give us the power to indulge

12 _____ on the spot. Once hooked, you might find it
(themselves, yourself, ourself, ourselves)

difficult to get along without a credit card.

Who's in Charge?

Interview with a Credit Counsellor

Exercise 1: Get Ready to Listen

Discuss these questions in a group.

1. Give the names of some credit cards.

2. What do you know about how credit cards work?

3. Name three situations in which it is common to use credit cards.

4. Do you think credit cards are a good idea?

5. What are some situations where it isn't a good idea to use credit cards?

6. In what emergency situations could credit cards be useful?

○ ○ **Exercise 2: Listen for Meaning**

Listen to the interview. Which of these things did you hear discussed?

1. credit card debt
2. the population of Canada
3. uses for credit cards
4. the coffee-shop business
5. different kinds of credit cards
6. why Jill M. spent too much money
7. how to avoid credit card debt
8. the correct way to use credit cards

○ ○ **Exercise 3: Listen for Details**

Listen to the interview. While you listen, answer the questions.

1. Who is Geoff Blake?
2. What is Mr. Blake going to talk about?
3. How much do Canadians owe on credit cards?
4. What happens when people use credit cards that doesn't happen when they pay cash?
5. Where can you hear horror stories about credit cards?
6. How much did Jill M. owe before she realized that she was in trouble?
7. What had she spent money on?
8. What good uses of credit cards are mentioned?
9. What advice does Mr. Blake offer about spending habits?
10. Name three ways people can keep track of what they spend.
11. What advice is offered about buying a jacket?
12. What does Mr. Blake say about large purchases?

Did You Know?   Credit card industry figures show that many people are delighted to pay higher interest rates for specialty cards. They like to be reminded of their favourite things, and will gladly pay more than they do for generic cards, as long as their cards are decorated with pictures of endangered animals or heroes such as Elvis Presley.

Lying, Cheating, and Stealing

Work in a group. Read the questions aloud. Each person should give his or his answer, and explain the reasons. Try to be honest!

1. You buy something in a store, and receive a dollar extra in change. You:

   a) tell the clerk

   b) pocket the change

2. At the subway, the ticket taker is away from the booth. You:

   a) pay anyway

   b) walk through without paying

3. You are having lunch with a friend. Your friend's lunch cost $2 more than yours. You:

   a) agree to split the bill evenly

   b) calculate what each of you owes, down to the last penny

4. You receive a bill from a department store. You notice that you were undercharged. The item cost $17.00, but you were charged only $7.00. You:

   a) pay the bill

   b) call the store to explain the error

5. Someone you know offers to sell you a radio. The price is much lower than in the store. You:

   a) buy the radio

   b) ask where he or she got the radio

   c) refuse on the grounds that it is probably "hot"

6. In a restaurant, the bill is incorrect. One dish is not included. You:

   a) tell the waiter or waitress

   b) pay the bill

7. You are buying a birthday gift for a family member. This person is very "tight" with money, and always gives you cheap gifts. You:

   a) buy something nice anyway, because you really like the person

   b) buy a gift similar to the one you usually receive

8. You want to get into a good restaurant, but it is very crowded. You:

   a) slip some money to the person in charge

   b) go to another restaurant

9. In a restaurant, when you are satisfied with the service, you generally:

   a) tip generously (more than 15 percent)

   b) tip about 15 percent

   c) tip the minimum amount (about 10 percent)

   d) leave a very small tip, or none at all

10. People are being asked to chip in money to buy a classmate or colleague a birthday present. The suggested amount is $5, but you are free to give whatever you want. You:

    a) give $5 or more

    b) give less than $5

    c) don't give anything

11. Someone at work asks you how much money you earn. You:

    a) tell the person that it's none of his or her business

    b) tell the person the true amount

    c) tell the person, but not the correct amount

12. Something you like is on sale. There is a big crowd in the store. You:

    a) leave: it's not worth the hassle

    b) wait patiently in line

    c) manoeuvre yourself to get what you want, pushing to the head of the line

13. You are invited to someone's house for dinner. You bring:

    a) something beautiful for the house

    b) an expensive cake or bottle of wine

    c) flowers

    d) a loaf of bread

    e) nothing

14. Someone calls from a local charity to ask for money. You:

    a) agree to give whatever you can

    b) say you can't give now, but you will try to give when you can

    c) slam down the phone

15. Payment for transportation can work on the honour system. If you get caught, you pay a large fine, but not many people get caught. When you take the bus, you:

    a) always pay

    b) sometimes pay

    c) never pay

Did You Know?   There are hundreds of languages in the world, but the dollar speaks them all.

Two Sides of the Coin

Work in a group. Read each statement aloud and discuss whether you agree or disagree with it. Explain why.

1. Money is the root of all evil.

2. A penny saved is a penny earned.

3. In this life, one thing counts—
   in the bank, large amounts.

4. Money can't buy you happiness.

5. Money won is twice as sweet as
   money earned.

6. I am willing to do anything for money, even work.

7. It is easier to make money than to save it: the first is
   exertion; the second, self-denial.

8. What's the good of money if you can't have a little fun with it?

9. It is easier to make money than to use it wisely.

10. Money makes the world go around.

Supplementary Grammar

Gerunds and Infinitives

Formation

A gerund is formed by adding "ing" to the base form of the verb.

Example: | **Verb** | **Gerund** |
| --- | --- |
| eat | eating |
| drink | drinking |
| buy | buying |

An infinitive is formed by using the base form of the verb after "to."

Example: | **Verb** | **Infinitive** |
| --- | --- |
| eat | to eat |
| drink | to drink |
| buy | to buy |

Usage

Both gerunds and infinitives function as nouns in a sentence. The gerund is used to follow some verbs. The infinitive is used to follow some verbs.

Example: I like rice. I like eating. I like to eat.

But: I enjoy rice.

I enjoy eating.

✗ I enjoy to eat.

✗ He wants having a peanut butter sandwich.

He wants to have a peanut butter sandwich

Some common verbs that are followed by the infinitive are listed below.

want to	promise to
need to	refuse to
pretend to	seem to
hope to	decide to
expect to	would like to

Exercise 1

Complete these sentences with the best verb. Use the infinitive form.

overeat   burn   leave   try   describe   come   order
be   take   have

1. The server advised the customers _____ dishes that weren't too spicy.
2. He didn't want us _____ our tongues on the hot food.
3. He said that he wanted the customers _____ the restaurant happy.
4. We expected the dishes _____ tasty but not too hot.
5. The restaurant owner invited us _____ a special dessert that wasn't on the menu.
6. She convinced everyone _____ a chance on her suggestion.
7. Someone in the group asked her _____ the ingredients.
8. She encouraged us _____ a second dessert free.
9. The server warned us not _____ just because the food was good.
10. We said we would advise our friends _____ to the restaurant.

Exercise 2

Find the sentences that have the wrong form of the verb. Write the correct form of the verb.

1. She would like having dessert after her meal.
2. He intends to order Chinese food for the party.
3. The waiter suggested trying the new dessert.
4. We agreed splitting the bill.
5. Everyone hoped to return to the restaurant.
6. Ray refused putting peanut butter sauce on his noodles.
7. Annabel would like to try something different from the menu.
8. Nobody seemed wanting to leave the table.
9. The group decided leaving a big tip.
10. The waiter seemed to be happy.

Exercise 3

Complete the sentences with the correct form of the verb.

1. People from San Francisco don't want _____ (pay for) their fortune cookies.
2. Nancy Anderson intends _____ (export) her fortune cookies to China in the future.

3. Customers in Chinese restaurants enjoy _____ (find) messages in their cookies.

4. The company that makes fortune cookies seems _____ (be) Japanese.

5. Mrs. Anderson promised _____ (deliver) her cookies in good condition.

6. Someone suggested _____ (wrap) the cookies in clear cellophane to protect them from dirt and humidity.

7. People who get messages in fortune cookies pretend _____ (believe) what they read.

8. The customers finished _____ (eat) their meal and ordered tea and cookies.

9. People in China usually expect _____ (find) a message in their fortune cookies.

10. They hope _____ (have) a message with good news about the future.

Conditional Sentences

Conditional I

Formation

A conditional sentence is made up of two clauses. The first type of conditional sentence (Conditional I) can be formed in two ways.

The "if" clause uses the present tense.

Example: If you are careful,

The main clause may use either the present tense or the future form.

Examples: If you are careful, you avoid accidents.

If you are careful, you will be safe.

Usage

The main clause uses the present tense when a habitual or factual situation is described.

Example: If you jump from the third floor, you risk serious injury.

If people are out in cold weather for a long time, they freeze.

The main clause uses the future form (will + verb) when a future activity is predicted.

Example: If you break your leg, a cast will be necessary.

Exercise 1

Choose the best verb to complete the sentence. Use the correct form of the verb.

take   be   smell   panic   arrive   yell   know   jump   occur   stay

1. If you _____, you will make poor decisions.
2. If there _____ a fire in the building, the best escape route is the stairs.
3. If you _____ what to do, you will make better decisions.
4. If people _____ calm, they improve their chances of escaping a fire.
5. If you _____ your key, you will be able to get back into your room.
6. If you _____ smoke, there is probably a fire somewhere.
7. If the fire-fighters _____ quickly, they will save lives.
8. If a fire _____, an alarm will alert you of danger.
9. If you _____ from the first floor, you will survive.
10. If someone _____ fire, everyone panics.

Exercise 2

Complete the sentences with the correct form of the verbs.

1. If the roads are icy, driving _____ (be) dangerous.
2. If you hit a patch of ice, you _____ (skid) out of control.
3. If you land in a snowbank, you _____ (be) lucky.
4. If the body temperature falls below 31 degrees, people usually _____ (die).
5. If you don't dress warmly in very cold weather, you _____ (risk) hypothermia.
6. If you leave the engine running, the car _____ (fill up) with carbon dioxide.
7. If the brain is without blood flow for four minutes, permanent damage _____ (occur).
8. If your skin is exposed to cold for a long time, you _____ (suffer) from frostbite.
9. If you find yourself in an emergency situation, you _____ (need) help.
10. If you stay in your car, rescuers usually _____ (find) you before too long.

Using Causative Verbs

Make, Have, Get

Formation

When "make" and "have" are used as causative verbs, they are followed by an object (the doer) and the base form of the main verb.

Examples: The personnel officer has candidates fill out an application form before their interviews.

When "get" is used as a causative verb, it is followed by an object (the doer) and the infinitive form of the main verb.

Example: That employee always gets someone else to do her work for her.

Usage

The verbs "make," "have," and "get" are causative when they have the sense to cause someone to do something. The subject is the causer that causes the doer to do something.

Example: The boss makes the accountant work overtime.
            (causer)   (doer)

Exercise 1

Choose the correct form of the verb to complete the sentences.

1. The director had the secretary _____ (bring) the CV.

2. The employees had the union representative _____ (explain) the labour code.

3. Sometimes interviewers make people _____ (answer) personal questions.

4. The negotiators got both sides _____ (agree) to a settlement.

5. The supervisor in our department makes us _____ (work) too hard.

6. The receptionist has everyone _____ (fill out) the same form.

7. The foreman got the employees _____ (work) harder by promising them a bonus.

8. We always have someone _____ (volunteer) to collect coffee money.

9. The volunteer makes a different person _____ (clean up) every week.

10. The union has each person _____ (sign) a card when he or she joins.

Exercise 2

Write sentences using each of the causative verbs ("have," "make," "get") correctly. Write two sentences for each verb.

Present Perfect Continuous

Formation

Use of the auxiliary verb "have" indicates the perfective aspect. This means you are making a statement that involves two different times.

For the present perfect, use the present form of the verb "have" and the past participle form of the verb that follows.

Example: Those trees have survived for hundreds of years.

Use of the auxiliary verb "be" indicates the continuous aspect. This means you wish to focus on the duration of an action.

Example: Loggers are cutting trees in the rain forest.

To form the present perfect continuous, use the present tense of the auxiliary verb "have," the past participle of the verb "be" and the continuous form of the main verb.

Example: Those trees have been growing along the coast as long as anyone can remember.

Usage I

Use the present perfect continuous to focus on the duration of an activity that began in the past and continues in the present (an action that is not completed).

Example: Those trees have been growing along the coast as long as anyone can remember.

(They began growing in the past and they continue growing today.)

Exercise 1

Complete the verb phrase in each sentence.

1. Scientists have been _____ (worry) about acid rain since the 1960s.

2. We _____ been breathing polluted air since the Industrial Revolution.

3. The hole in the ozone layer _____ been growing from year to year.

4. The cutting and burning of tropical rain forests has been _____ (contribute) to changes in the climate.

5. Companies have _____ dumping toxic chemicals into our rivers for years.

6. Efforts to clean up the environment _____ been increasing as people have become aware of the problem.

7. The mountain of trash on Staten Island has been _____ (grow) for many years.

8. New laws have _____ helping to protect the environment for future generations.

9. School programmes to involve young people in environmental awareness have been _____ (make) progress.

10. The public _____ been putting pressure on governments to protect the environment.

Usage II

Do not use the present perfect continuous form of the verb to describe events in indefinite past time. Use the present perfect.

Example: ✘ He has been seeing that movie on acid rain three times.

                ✔ He has seen that movie on acid rain three times.

Exercise 1

Choose the correct form of the verb (present perfect or present perfect continuous). If both are possible, write "either."

1. The amount of carbon dioxide in the atmosphere _____ (increase) 20 percent in the last 200 years.

2. Fossil fuel use _____ (contribute) to the problem of atmospheric pollution since the invention of the car.

3. People _____ (notice) the damage caused by acid rain and asking for government action.

4. In some parts of the world people_____ (live) side by side with nature for centuries.

5. Millions of species _____ (disappear) in recent years.

6. Environmental protection agencies _____ (prevent) some kinds of industrial pollution from continuing.

7. The destruction of rain forests _____ (attract) more and more attention lately.

8. Many North Americans _____ (begin) to be less wasteful.

9. Several recent oil spills _____ (focus) public attention on the need for care in transporting oil by sea.

10. The number of oil spills _____ (increase) for some time.

Conditional Sentences

Conditional II

Formation

A conditional sentences is made up of two clauses. In the second type of conditional sentence (Conditional II), the "if" clause uses the simple past tense.

Examples: If I took a long vacation,

If I knew someone in Vancouver,

The main clause uses the modal auxiliary "would" and the base form of the main verb.

Examples: If I took a long vacation, I would visit Halifax.

If I knew people in Vancouver, I would stay with them.

Usage

The Conditional II sentence describes a hypothetical situation related to the present and future.

Examples: If I took a long vacation, I would visit Halifax.

(I have only a short vacation, so I will not visit Halifax.)

If I knew their names, I would introduce them.

(I do not know their names, so I will not introduce them.)

Exercise 1

Complete the clause with the correct form of the verb.

1. If I lost my passport in a foreign country, I _____ (go) to my embassy.

2. If I visited a tropical country, I _____ (need) shots.

3. If I had a lot of money, I _____ (travel) first class.

4. If I missed my plane, I _____ (have) a big problem.

5. If I bought a new camera, I _____ (buy) a Nikon.

6. If I knew where my umbrella was, I _____ (get) it myself.

7. If I had a choice of holiday destinations, I _____ (choose) a hot country.

8. If I went to Cairo, I _____ (stop over) in Rome.

9. If the airline lost my luggage, I _____ (be) angry.

10. If someone stole my wallet in the airport, I _____ (contact) the police immediately.

Exercise 2

Complete the sentence with the correct form of the verb.

1. If you _____ (arrive) too late, you would disturb people.

2. People would be angry if you _____ (wake) them up in the middle of the night.

3. Nobody would say anything if you _____ (use) the telephone for a local call.

4. If you called long distance, there _____ (be) objections.

5. If you _____ (use) up all the hot water, the host would be furious.

6. You would be unwelcome if you _____ (eat) all the food in the refrigerator.

7. If you volunteered to cook a meal, you _____ (make) a good impression.

8. People _____ (feel) uncomfortable if you invaded their privacy.

9. If guests _____ (stay) too long, they would be a nuisance.

10. If you were late for dinner, you _____ (call) to let people know.

Exercise 3

Write three sentences describing what a good guest would do in different situations.

Conditional III

Formation

In the third type of conditional sentence (Conditional III), the "if" clause uses the past perfect form of the verb.

Examples: If I had saved more money,

If we had made reservations,

The main clause uses the modal auxiliary "would" with the present perfect form of the main verb.

Examples: If I had saved more money, I would have gone to Paris.

If we had made reservations, we would have had a better room at the hotel.

Usage

A Conditional III sentence describes a hypothetical situation in the past.

Example: If I had saved enough money, I would have gone to Paris.

(I didn't save enough money so I didn't visit Paris.)

Exercise 1

Complete the clauses with the correct form of the verb.

1. If anyone had stayed awake for the whole flight, they _____ (be) very tired when they arrived.

2. If pillows had been available, I _____ (ask) for one.

3. If I had known how long the flight was, I _____ (request) a stopover.

4. If that passenger hadn't been late, the flight _____ (leave) on time.

5. If the airline had offered a choice of schedules, the tourists _____ (prefer) a later flight.

6. If my company had given me a choice, I _____ (choose) to fly business class.

7. If we had missed the connection, the airline _____ (pay) for a hotel.

8. If the in-flight movie had been better, more people _____ (watch) it.

9. If she had been afraid of flying, she _____ (go) by train.

10. If they had known that the time zone was different, they _____ (reset) their watches.

Exercise 2

Complete the sentences with the correct form of the verbs.

1. If I had known about the mosquitoes, I _____ (stay) at home.

2. I would have brought sunscreen with me if I _____ (think) of it.

3. I _____ (go) swimming if the water had been warmer.

4. If my friends had come, it _____ (be) more fun.

5. If it had been cheaper, they _____ (stay) a week longer.

6. She would have written more often, if she _____ (have) time.

7. If the weather _____ (be) warmer, we would have enjoyed our holiday more.

8. We _____ (ask) for air conditioning if we had known about the climate there.

9. If the tour had left later, we _____ (join) it.

10. If we _____ (speak) the language better, we would have asked more questions.

Exercise 3

Write three sentences about hypothetical past situations.

Expressing Future Time

Using Present Simple Form

To indicate a scheduled event (in the future), it is possible to use the simple present form.

Example: Our plane leaves in the morning.

Exercise 1

Identify the expressions of time. Then, choose the best verb from the list below to complete each sentence.

leave   arrive   open   close   start   finish   begin

end   come   return   stop

1. The parking lot _____ at 8:00.
2. The office _____ at 9:00.
3. The next candidate _____ at 10:30.
4. The buses _____ running at midnight.
5. The fund-raising campaign _____ next week.
6. Jane _____ from her holidays in a week.
7. Mike _____ his new job on Monday.
8. The campaign _____ at the end of the month.
9. The students don't _____ until September.
10. Classes _____ in April.

Exercise 2

Write five sentences about future events using the present simple tense.

Using Present Continuous Form

To indicate a planned event (in the future), it is possible to use the present continuous form. When the present continuous is used to express future time, a time marker is required.

Examples: We are taking a special course next month.

I am seeing her in August.

In sentences that have time clauses, use the simple present tense in the time clause and the present continuous form in the main clause to indicate future time.

Time clauses begin with expressions such as:

when   before   after   as soon as   until

Examples: After we hear his report, we are having a lunch break.

As soon as we finish lunch, we are returning to the office.

Exercise 1

Complete the sentences with the appropriate verb tense for each clause.

1. After they _____ (finish) work, they are heading home.
2. As soon as I win the lottery, I _____ (quit) my job.
3. Della is moving the car before she _____ (get) a ticket.
4. Until I _____ (know) why she asked, I am not answering.
5. When the coffee break starts, someone _____ (serve) coffee.
6. I'm not saying anything until the meeting _____ (starts).
7. As soon as 5 o'clock _____ (come), the employees are leaving.
8. I'm applying for a new job after I _____ (get) my diploma.
9. Nobody _____ (get) a raise until profits increase.
10. I'm taking my holidays as soon as I _____ (have) permission.

Exercise 2

Complete the sentences with the appropriate verb tense for each clause.

1. I _____ (take) a trip when I _____ (retire) from my job.
2. After they _____ (finish) the course, they _____ (get) new assignments.
3. As soon as summer _____(come), we _____ (change) to a shorter work week.
4. Until I _____ (hear) both sides, I _____ (keep) an open mind.
5. We _____ (make) a decision when we _____ (know) more about it.
6. The company _____ (close) when the vacation period _____ (start).
7. She _____ (take) courses as soon as she _____ (get) permission.
8. Before they _____ (ship) the merchandise, they _____ (check) their order file.
9. I _____ (stay) here until I _____ (find) a better job.
10. After I _____ (complete) this report, I _____ (take) a rest.

Irregular Past Tense and Past Participle Forms

arise	arose	arisen	get	got	got (gotten)
be	was, were	been	give	gave	given
bear	bore	born	go	went	gone
beat	beat	beaten	grind	ground	ground
become	became	become	grow	grew	grown
begin	began	begun	hang	hung	hung (hanged)
bend	bent	bent	have	had	had
bet	bet	bet	hear	heard	heard
bite	bit	bitten	hide	hid	hidden
bleed	bled	bled	hit	hit	hit
blow	blew	blown	hold	held	held
break	broke	broken	hurt	hurt	hurt
bring	brought	brought	keep	kept	kept
build	built	built	know	knew	known
buy	bought	bought	lay	laid	laid
catch	caught	caught	lead	led	led
choose	chose	chosen	leap	leapt (leaped)	leapt (leaped)
come	came	come	leave	left	left
cost	cost	cost	lend	lent	lent
cut	cut	cut	let	let	let
dig	dug	dug	lie	lay	lain
dive	dove (dived)	dived	lie	lied	lied
do	did	done	lose	lost	lost
draw	drew	drawn	make	made	made
drink	drank	drunk	mean	meant	meant
drive	drove	driven	meet	met	met
eat	ate	eaten	pay	paid	paid
fall	fell	fallen	put	put	put
feed	fed	fed	quit	quit	quit
feel	felt	felt	read	read	read
fight	fought	fought	ride	rode	ridden
find	found	found	ring	rang	rung
fit	fit	fit	rise	rose	risen
flee	fled	fled	run	ran	run
fly	flew	flown	say	said	said
forbid	forbade	forbidden	see	saw	seen
forget	forgot	forgotten	sell	sold	sold
forgive	forgave	forgiven	send	sent	sent
freeze	froze	frozen	set	set	set
fry	fried	fried	shake	shook	shaken

shine	shone	shone	string	strung	strung
shoot	shot	shot	swear	swore	sworn
show	showed	shown	sweep	swept	swept
shrink	shrank	shrunk	swim	swam	swum
shut	shut	shut	swing	swung	swung
sing	sang	sung	take	took	taken
sink	sank	sunk	teach	taught	taught
sit	sat	sat	tear	tore	torn
sleep	slept	slept	tell	told	told
slide	slid	slid	think	thought	thought
speak	spoke	spoken	throw	threw	thrown
spend	spent	spent	try	tried	tried
spin	spun	spun	understand	understood	understood
spit	spat	spat	wake	woke	woken
spread	spread	spread	wear	wore	worn
stand	stood	stood	weave	wove	woven
steal	stole	stolen	win	won	won
stick	stuck	stuck	wind	wound	wound
sting	stung	stung	wring	wrung	wrung
strike	struck	struck	write	wrote	written

Verbs Followed by Gerunds

admit	delay	go + an activity	practise	stop
advise	deny	imagine	quit	suggest
anticipate	discuss	keep	recall	understand
appreciate	dislike	mention	recommend	
avoid	enjoy	mind	report	
complete	finish	miss	resist	
consider	give up	postpone	risk	

Verbs Followed by Infinitives

afford	decide	hope	promise	wait
agree	expect	learn	refuse	want
appear	fail	manage	regret	wish
ask	forget	need	remember	
care	hesitate	pretend	seem	

Community Contact Tasks

In the Community

Task #1

The Library Task

In Class

Work in a group. Make a list of questions you can ask in the library to get information about:

  a) lending policies

  b) services

  c) special events

In the Community

Work with a partner. Visit a library. Ask your questions.

Reporting Back

Work in a group. Share your information.

In the Community

Task #2

The Food Task

In Class

Work in a group. Make a list of unusual or exotic foods that are available in your city or town. Discuss which restaurants or stores in your area might have these foods.

Make a list of questions to find out the following:

      a) what the food looks like and tastes like

      b) where the food comes from

      c) how the food is prepared

      d) special customs associated with the food, or special ways to eat it

In the Community

Work with a partner. Interview three people. Find out about some of the foods on your list.

Reporting Back

Work in a group. Share your information.

In the Community

Task #3

The Job Task

In Class

Work in a group. Make a list of jobs that interest you. Discuss where you could find information about these jobs.

In the Community

Work with a partner. Go to a Canada Employment Centre. Ask questions to find out about jobs that are available and qualifications needed for these jobs.

Reporting Back

Work in a group. Discuss your information.

In the Community

Task #4

The Environment Task

In Class

Work in a group. Make a list of places to which you can send a letter to express your concern about the environment or to get more information on what you can do to help the environment. Use these categories to help you:

 a) an environmental group: to get more information on what you can do

 b) a company: to express satisfaction or dissatisfaction with how a product or its packaging affects the environment

 c) a government official or agency (for example, the environment minister): to ask for information on specific policies such as plans to deal with ozone depletion

In the Community

Work with a partner.

1. Find the telephone number and address of one suitable company, group, or agency from the phone book.

2. Call the company, group, or agency to find out who is responsible for dealing with environmental concerns.

3. Write a letter to express your opinion or to get information.

Reporting Back

Work in a group. Exchange letters to get feedback from others. Then send the letters.

In the Community

Task #5

The Visitors Task

In Class:

Make a list of questions you can ask someone about his or her experiences of having visitors or being a visitor in someone else's home.

In the Community

Work with a partner. Interview three people. Ask your questions. Find out about funny or annoying experiences people have had as hosts or as visitors. Find out about good experiences they have had.

Reporting Back

Work in a group. Share your stories.

In the Community

Task #6

The Night Work Task

In Class

Work in a group.

1. Make a list of occupations that people do at night.
2. Write questions to ask people who work at night. Aim to find out what the people do in their jobs and how they feel about their work.

In the Community

Work with a partner. Interview two people who work at night. Ask your questions. Get as many details as you can.

Reporting Back

Work in a group. Share your information.

In the Community

Task #7

The Comic Strip Task

In Class

Bring the comic pages from some newspapers to class.

Work in a group. Make a list of the comic strips that deal with family situations. Choose three strips. Discuss the following information for each comic strip:

    a) the characters in the family

    b) the role each person has

    c) the kind of situations that the comic strip deals with

Follow the comic strips for a few days at home.

In the Community

Work with a partner. Interview three people. Ask them which comic strips they prefer, and why. Get as many details as you can.

Reporting Back

Work in a group. Share your information. Make a chart that includes information from the class. Which comic strips are most popular?

Option: Write a letter to the creator of a comic strip, giving reasons why you like the comic.

In the Community

Task #8

The Credit Card Task

In Class

Work in a group. Make a list of different types of credit cards and places where you can apply for credit cards.

In the Community

Work with a partner. Visit two of the places on your list. Ask questions about obtaining the cards. Get information about interest rates and fees.

Reporting Back

Work in a group. Compare your information. Which credit cards offer the best deals?

هذا الكتاب ممتع و شيّق

如果你读了过本台 你会感到"绝3"、太棒3！让人难以忘记。

ESTE LIBRO ES MUY INTERESANTE ! BUENA SUERTE!!!

英語は易しい.
この本は面白い
さようなら.

Ce livre est très intéressant !

excellent pour apprendre !

BONJOUR

TSARA ITY BOKY ITY . VELOMA

Ce n'est qu'un début...

Este livro é muito interessante

HAS ARRIVAT FINS ACÍ, MOLT BÉ NANO!